I0074413

Cures for Ailing Organizations

Revive Your Organization and Keep It Healthy

Sue Knaup

Publisher's Cataloging-in-Publication data
Knaup, Sue.
    Cures for ailing organizations : revive your organization and
keep it healthy / Sue Knaup.
        p. cm.
    ISBN 978-0-9859889-2-0
    Includes bibliographical references and index.

    1. Nonprofit organizations --Management. 2. Organizational
effectiveness. 3. Organizational behavior. 4. Performance.   I.
Title.

HD62.6 .K58 2014
658.4/012 --dc23   2014952048

Copyright © 2014 by Sue Knaup

All rights reserved. No portion of this book may be
reproduced for large-scale production, posting to the
internet, sales or distribution, by any process or technique,
without the express written permission of the publisher.
However, worksheets and samples may be reproduced in
small quantities for educational and training purposes as
long as this book is clearly referenced.

Printed in the United States of America

First Edition

ISBN 978-0-9859889-2-0

One Street Press
P.O. Box 3309
Prescott, Arizona 86302
USA

www.onestreet.org

To Mimi, my grandmother,
who got me mixed up in organizations in the first place.

Table of Contents

Section 1: Diagnosing Ailments

Section 2: First Aid and Remedies

Section 3: Getting Healthy

Preface
About This Book and Its Author

The norm for most organizations founded for social good has become toil and strife, infighting and eventual failure. In 2010 the Internal Revenue Service (IRS) provided an astonishing snapshot for the United States when it began revoking the charitable status of nearly 300,000 organizations for failure to report. The number of U.S. registered nonprofits had ballooned to more than 1.5 million, so about one of every five had derailed. As more register, many accomplish nothing yet still report. Countries around the world are seeing a similar phenomenon.

Unlike for-profit corporations, where failure is a disgrace, nonprofits are expected to struggle. It's a sad irony that our society abandons compassionate, selfless organizations yet embraces those focused entirely on monetary gain. I suspect this has more to do with the lack of a pertinent support system for nonprofits and social enterprises than a conscious choice to favor greed. This book aims to inspire a support system that will lift nonprofits to higher expectations.

I was privileged to work for healthy nonprofits starting at a very young age. Each had vibrant purposes and exciting programs that attracted countless supporters and brought in ample funding. They trained us (volunteers and staff) toward great achievements and paid all their staff well. When I inevitably encountered dysfunctional organizations, they seemed bizarre to me. Little did I know that the first nonprofits I had worked for were the anomalies.

As I fortunately learned early on, healthy organizations do exist, but most were launched and are led by exceptional individuals. If we step back and look at our whole world for just a minute, we can see it's got more than its share of problems. In this world of growing poverty, disease, exploitation of animals and people, and devastation of natural resources, we've got a heck of a lot of work to do to clean up the mess. Yet the organizations tasked with this work seem incapable of functioning without an extraordinary human being at their helm. Martin Luther King Jr., Mohandas Gandhi, Nelson Mandela, Mother Teresa—they make us sigh with admiration and hope that their clone will respond to our executive director job announcement. But waiting for their clones to arrive and chastising those who do not fit their mold only add to the dysfunction of our organizations.

It's time to reshape our expectations, to look at our organizations as bodies that suffer from ailments and common diseases that can be treated and brought back to health. No magic pill, no extraordinary person, will cure an ailing organization. We, the ordinary folks, must stand up and work together building our organizations the hard way, as a team. This is the healthy way that will grow the strong bones and muscles to stride ahead toward great changes in our lives and communities, whether we have the next Mother Teresa on our team or not.

For-profit corporations do not rely on superheroes. While we must avoid their self-centered indulgence, I say it's time to recognize their success and start tending to beneficial organizations they can compete with those designed for profits only. Ordinary people can create extraordinary organizations simply by responding to common danger signs and focusing on healthy, effective habits. In three sections, this book presents the response system I've refined over my four decades working with organizations. The first section deals with diagnosis. The middle section offers first aid and remedy procedures. The last section will show you how to lift your organization into health and keep it there.

You will learn about organization ailments and crises including common hazards that so often lead good people to do very bad things. While criminal acts such as theft and property destruction will be included as hazards, most of the ailments that bring organizations to their knees are legal, however damaging they may be. Many of these threats are obvious:

- New leaders, rogue staff members, or factions are overriding decisions, tearing the organization apart, and attempting to change it to serve their personal needs.
- There is not enough money for payroll or to pay bills.
- People within the organization are badmouthing it to the media, officials, and the general public.
- The organization has developed a bad reputation in its community.
- The number of board members has dwindled and because the organization has been in crisis for so long, no new board members can be found.

Leaders in such situations often panic; they know how close they are to disaster. The first section of this book is designed to bring the calm of understanding to such terrifying circumstances. However, most emergencies result from deceptively simple deviations that would have been easily remedied, but are too often ignored. A few examples include:

- Each leader is working in a different direction without any agreed-upon work plan or budget.
- Leaders are confused over roles. For instance, the executive director is not seeking the board's input on policy, or board members are giving orders to staff on daily tasks.
- Contractors have been given the power to influence the organization's direction.
- The board has skipped meetings, the executive director feels isolated, and the staff is operating without direction.

- Earmarked program or project funds have been used for operating costs and the funders left in the dark.
- Leaders, desperate for funding, have accepted money for a project outside the organization's mission, thus alienating their core supporters.
- Leaders do not know the mission of the organization.

In fact, the only sign you need to determine that an organization is ailing, and potentially facing a serious crisis, is that it no longer can focus its energy toward achieving its mission (also known as its purpose). Every one of the previous symptoms diverts energy away from an organization's purpose. Until now, too many leaders who have found themselves in such situations have had to face their crisis alone.

This book presents a new expectation—that these dilemmas are not unusual and that anyone can help restore an organization to health. You will not find here the quick fixes or isolated exercises that dominate most nonprofit management books. Instead, prepare yourself and your team for a comprehensive process that will uncover the likely causes of trouble, show you how to confront each problem with proven solutions, and set you on a path toward continued organization health. You will learn how to listen to leaders in crisis and help them find solutions. You will gain the skills to reconnect warring factions to once again work together for great causes. And you will come to realize that restoring health to important organizations will be worth the effort it demands.

At this point, you might ask why you should bother saving or even creating an organization if they are so prone to upheavals. Why not tackle problems as an individual? This is a valid question and one you should ask before embarking on the arduous journey. I cover this early in the book and even offer disbanding as the treatment for organizations suffering from an overbearing leader. If you are ambitious, outgoing, and committed to a single product or program that will help this world, you may not need an organization as your backdrop. Form a sole proprietorship to give your product a name and management structure and go for it.

An organization is not about one product or program. An organization brings together many people with many different perspectives who all agree that a particular and significant change must happen for their community, whether it is a neighborhood, an entire city, or a global community where people are bound by shared interest rather than by geography. Leaders of healthy organizations expect such a change to take place over many years, if not generations. While all who participate bring their own perspectives and ideas, each one knows precisely what the desired change is and can articulate it without having to refer to written documents. Perhaps their town suffers from racism so they have come together to stop it. Such a massive shift from an ingrained societal norm cannot happen in a short period. Even when appreciation and respect for everyone in that community does finally become the norm, the organization will have to remain in order to prevent racism from returning. Any significant change worth fighting for must be protected once it is won. No individual can cause significant changes alone. Even if that were possible, a human life is not long enough to protect something that is truly important to future generations.

Leaders of healthy organizations cherish input from their team as well as from anyone interested in their work. They even reach out to opponents to discover ways to refine their programs to appeal to the broadest audience. They value contrary viewpoints as their means of examining all angles of any proposal. The people who flock to healthy organizations bring not only their unique ideas and experiences, but also their personal networks. They tell everyone they know about the organization and encourage them to participate.

This book emphasizes the value of the people that make up organizations. It shows readers how to identify danger signs and react immediately to anyone who does their organization harm. Readers will find a new expectation of health and vitality for organizations contributing to society and zero tolerance for bad behavior, infighting, and strife. Nonprofit leaders will find praise for profits. Social entrepreneurs will tap into healthy organization structures that will move them past single product goals.

I wrote this book over the past 16 years if you count frustrated notes scribbled on scrap paper and thrown into various files. It started in 1997 when I helped found a local bicycle and pedestrian nonprofit here in Prescott, Arizona called Prescott Alternative Transportation (PAT). At the time, I owned and operated a for-profit bike shop, which I'd founded six years earlier. Founding a business was a breeze, at least as far as forms and filing went. I had at least three business mentor organizations to tap through our Chamber of Commerce and community college. Their advice was straightforward and easy to follow, concepts like inventory control, cash flow, and how to read profit-and-loss statements. When I opened the doors, all of my customers fully understood what the bike shop was and what they could expect from shopping there.

Founding PAT was not so easy. The nonprofit incorporation forms and filing were a convoluted mess. PAT was the first organization I had incorporated. Every person with nonprofit experience I spoke with gave me different advice. The only consistencies were in IRS language regarding the use of funds. There was no expectation to succeed or achieve great things, just an expectation to not steal money. I found a pro bono attorney and CPA and worked with them to file the paperwork. I figured the rest would come from my fellow founding board members as we focused on our mission of a bicycle and pedestrian friendly community. Sure enough, that's how we built a healthy organization that continues its important work today.

Since founding PAT, I've worked with leaders of bicycle organizations all over the world. Bicycles are like canaries to me. They reveal the health and priorities of any community. You can determine whether a community values diversity or oppression just by noticing how many and what sort of people are riding bikes. Thriving communities always have many people of all ages, income levels, and ethnicities cycling through their streets. That's why, after working in the fields of animal rights, environment, and special populations I finally landed on bicycle advocacy as my chosen cause. But as I reached beyond PAT to discover where the bicycle advocacy movement was succeeding, I was dismayed to find it infested with the same dysfunction I had found was common in the nonprofit world.

That's why in 2007 I founded One Street as an international nonprofit that helps the leaders of bicycle advocacy organizations avoid common missteps that cripple the movement. Any leader of any bicycle organization, no matter where they are in the world, can contact us anytime for advice and to connect with the resources they need. While these bicycle organizations were foremost in my mind as I wrote this book, I also tapped my work with many different movements so that what I offer will resonate with any leader of any organization working to help their chosen community.

I am also very enthusiastic about social enterprise because it melds for-profit business sense with an expectation for social benefit. After 40 years working for and leading nonprofits and 13 years as a for-profit bike shop owner, I am ready to see the best of both combined.

The first organization I worked for was a small nonprofit group tracking and cataloging all the street trees in my neighborhood in Mill Valley, California. My great-grandfather, Frank Bostwick, was one of the founders of the town, its first mayor, and its first banker. My grandmother, Helen Bostwick, whom I called Mimi, got me into the street tree group. I'll never forget the bittersweet taste of power when a tree I had identified as diseased was cut down the next day. I was ten years old. That tree has been a constant reminder of the grave responsibility all of us hold when we take up any leadership position.

The next organization Mimi got me into was the Marin County Humane Society. She was a founder of that organization as well as the Mill Valley Tennis Club. I suspect I've got a lot of

Mimi's blood in me because we both see solutions in the form
of organizations. But even as her granddaughter, I had to wait to
reach the humane society's minimum age of 12 for volunteers.
I counted the days. I was overwhelmed with pride the day I was
finally accepted and sewed the official humane society patches
onto my work shirt. The employees I worked with showed me how
to speak to the abused animals I cared for, even if my gut churned
with disgust at the ticks and sores that covered them. My words
soothed them and they even seemed to laugh at my impromptu
jokes and tales. My second year there, I won their annual award
for service toward animal protection and welfare (Mimi attended
the ceremony) and by age 16 I was a full-time employee. The
unconditional respect and dignity we gave to those animals flows
over to every creature I have worked with since and feeds my
affection for any organization that sets out to stop the abuse and
oppression of any living being.

     That humane society job led me to two other nonprofit
gigs—at the Marin Wildlife Center (now Wildcare) and the Fund
for Animals. Between the ages of 12 and 16 I divided my time
between the three. At the Fund for Animals, I was given the
responsibility of organizing massive rallies on Union Square in San
Francisco against the fur trade. I also became a regular lobbyist
with the Fund's small lobbying team in Sacramento, fighting for
and winning bills to stop useless scientific research on animals, ban
the steel-jaw trap, protect predators, and banish the decompression
chamber used to euthanize animals. One of my fellow lobbyists
was Gladys Sargent, part owner of the Oakland Raiders and
prominent voice for animals at the Capitol, who taught me that
the real lobbying took place across the street in a dark, smoky
bar. I'd sip a soda as Gladys negotiated with the senators and
assemblymen.

     My Fund for Animals and wildlife center connections
led me to a few short gigs with environmental nonprofits
including Greenpeace before discovering Friends of the River, an
organization working to save the Stanislaus River near Yosemite.

A dam had been built and the rising waters were turning rolling hills into islands where wild animals were trapped. The Stanislaus Wildlife Rescue Program was the first organization I founded, complete with board of directors, funder reports, and annual budget. It was 1979. I was 15. I led my helpers on countless canoe trips to those shrinking islands where we scooped up squirrels, rabbits, wood rats, mice, and rattlesnakes to set free on the retreating shoreline. Many of my helpers were river guides who introduced me to rafting through the Stanislaus' sheer limestone canyon, a playground of whitewater, side-canyon waterfalls and swimming holes I soon fell in love with. Friends of the River could not save the Stanislaus, but the group went on to become the nation's top river advocacy organization as it now protects all of California's rivers from the fate suffered by the Stanislaus. The loss of the Stanislaus River broke my heart. That scar reminds me to this day of the significance of every detail of every campaign, especially early response.

After that heartbreak, I ran away from advocacy and followed some of my new river guide friends into a career that spanned 18 summers guiding people with disabilities and special needs on wilderness river adventures, mostly in Utah and the Grand Canyon. That's where I learned to question first impressions, where guides and clients became equals, just a group of people making their way down a river. Splore is one of the nonprofits I worked for in this field and I feature them later in this book. Also in this book, you will notice the influence of another sort of training I had to go through as a river guide for special populations—first aid and eventually emergency medical technician (EMT). Medical response is surprisingly similar to the response steps needed to treat distressed organizations.

My departure from advocacy nonprofits also opened doors into worldwide adventures, farm and commercial fishing jobs, and my job as a San Francisco bicycle messenger. I rode as a messenger each winter, complementing my summer river guide life and my dual adoration of bicycles and boats. When I was finally mowed down by a Cadillac after seven winters, the workers comp insurance helped me to train as a bicycle mechanic. I then opened my own bike shop here in Prescott, where I'd attended Prescott College and become smitten with the town. After six years listening to my customers complain about the danger of riding a bicycle or even walking along Prescott's streets, I realized I had to do something. I braved my past and the still painful loss of the Stanislaus and founded PAT to advocate for streets where even the most vulnerable traveler would be welcome.

So that's the journey to here, a path lit by some of the best nonprofits and nonprofit leaders to grace this world. They are my beacons every time I answer a One Street call from a leader in crisis. But I must say that the organization leaders I've helped to guide out of danger are truly the heroes of this book. They are the ones who confronted the worst human behavior, witnessed atrocities against their fellow leaders, and emerged to tell about it. Each of the heart-pounding calls and emailed pleas comes from someone who could have easily walked away, but instead chose to fight for their organization's life. These courageous leaders have helped me formulate the methods of response and prove the steps that guide struggling organizations back to health.

I expect that most readers will be leaders of organizations, so I have presented concepts throughout this book from this perspective. However, anyone who wants to help an ailing organization will find what they need in these pages, even if they have to adapt some of the information to their non-leadership perspective.

So, let's find out what is ailing your organization.

Section
1

Diagnosis

Chapter 1
Healthy Organizations

Healthy organizations are easy to spot. We want to give them a call to see how we can help. Their articles in newspapers, blogs, and magazines make us read to the end in hopes of finding a call to action we can take part in. People we respect ask if we are a member. So how did they get there and how do they maintain such a healthy glow about them?

I have found that organizations are astonishingly similar to any organism, especially a human being. Any organization, much like a living creature, depends on complex, interdependent systems. The people, programs, and policies of an organization must all work in unison, much like the circulatory, respiratory, and nervous systems, otherwise the entire organism will shut down and die. The physical structure of an organization, like the skeleton and muscles of a person, also plays an important role in its health. Organizations are made up of organisms, that is, humans. So these similarities should not be surprising. You will find this analogy woven throughout this book. Healthy organizations, much like healthy organisms, have a clear focus on their purpose and share these basic traits:

- There is a balance between the energy they consume and the energy they give out;
- Many people of many types and talents are assisting with their activities;
- They have a clear, single-sentence mission

statement that shows what they do, where they do it, and for whom;

- They are admired and supported by the community they serve;
- They follow effective policies and procedures;
- Their external communications are frequent and well received; and
- Their internal communications keep leaders and staff updated and inspired.

As we begin, I want to emphasize balance. Open most books or websites on organization development and you will find tantalizingly simple tasks meant to fix your organization. Actually, you and your fellow leaders will have to work hard not only to diagnose your troubles, but to maintain a balanced health once you've set your organization back on track. There are no magic pills or quick fixes. Just as we do for ourselves, you will have to learn about good nutrition, proper exercise, and how to control your organization's particular chronic health issues. You also need to assess your environment, the amount of stress your team can withstand, and—don't snicker—what makes all of you happy.

1.1 Body Structure Analogy

BALANCE: Healthy organizations find and retain a balance that suits their particular purpose. They are never larger or smaller than they need to be to reach their goals. The people who spend their time with them enjoy a balance between effort and accomplishment. They can see the results of their work and this feeds their desire to continue.

Organizations need a balance of exercise and nutrition; that is, energy output matches energy input. Are you and your team spending your days on tedious administrative duties or responding to attacks rather than following a calm plan toward your purpose? That's not healthy exercise; it can't cause positive and lasting change.

Like nutritious food, the people and partners that contribute time and resources to your organization bring far more nutrients than meet the eye. Seeking only funding without considering the people behind the contribution is like craving sugary snacks. Developing partners, communicating with members, and creating a volunteer system can look a lot like eating our Brussels sprouts, but these activities bring our organizations the nutrients they need.

The point is to balance exercise and healthy nutrient input with necessary daily duties. Just as no single management exercise will cure your ailments, no single healthy habit will revive your organization. Without a balance of hard work and fun, organizations become vulnerable to sudden injuries and ailments as well as diseases that creep in over time.

PEOPLE: I see people as an organization's muscles. When you think of healthy organizations, people will always come to mind—the leaders, your favorite employees, and your friends who are members and meet you at their events. Ailing organizations often have people working in opposite directions or even against each other, sapping their strength. In contrast, healthy organizations have a large number and variety of people all working in unison toward the same purpose.

Some must take responsibility as leaders of the organization. Just like the major muscles of the legs, abdomen, and back, leaders hold an organization up and ensure it can withstand unexpected blows. Other people are also important, but without leadership they will not know where to put their energy. Not only do the leaders need titles, they need to be visible to their supporters, officials, and the general public as the embodiment of the organization. Without leaders who take pride in their responsibility for the organization's health, the organization will crumble. I've witnessed this too often with organizations that were founded by a large group of people, none of whom stepped up to lead. The worst thing about these situations is that without leaders, there is no one to contact even to offer help.

PURPOSE: Muscles need a skeleton to attach to. That's the purpose of the organization, captured in its mission statement. Healthy organizations always have a clear and concise mission statement, most often one sentence long, that states exactly what the organization does, where it works, and for whom. But a clear and concise mission statement is not enough. The purpose needs to match the appropriate level of impact its founders envisioned. If the organization is a social club, the purpose will be to bring certain people together in a particular community. If it's an organization that's meant to cause significant and lasting change, the mission statement must pronounce that change with powerful, clear language that cannot be misinterpreted. The mission statement holds the organization's form through all the twists and turns of life. If a mission statement is explained in different ways by different people, the organization will flop and tumble to the whim of whoever comes along.

Did Nelson Mandela and the African National Congress (ANC) call for a gentle easing of apartheid, perhaps on weekends and holidays? No! They called for the *end* of apartheid, the *end* of racial segregation in South Africa. Period. While the ANC had been working for civil rights during their first 36 years, their struggle against apartheid started in earnest in the mid-1940s and consumed the entire focus of the ANC for nearly 50 years. After the fall of apartheid in the early 1990s, they adjusted their structure to become a major political party in South Africa still dedicated to equality of all South Africans. This shows the potential evolution of any organization that becomes healthy and stays that way. The ANC may not look the same as it did 100 years ago, but the healthy skeleton (purpose) that it was born with remains.

Consider whether your organization's purpose is strong enough to carry it through generations of positive change. A strong purpose will meet criteria similar to those planned for a campaign or a new product:

- The change is easily understood and desired in the target community.

- The change will eventually be perceived by most people as better than the status quo.
- Many people in the community care about the change and some are passionate about it.

Of course, not everyone will support the purpose of a healthy organization. In fact, if everyone supported it, there would be no need for it. Opponents are expected. But supporters are, too. If the purpose of your organization is too vague, too boring, or too exclusive, very few of your potential supporters and future leaders will come forward to help. Without a large number and variety of people actively involved in the organization, it will not have the muscles to get anything done.

PUBLIC IMAGE: Skin inhibits invasions from substances that would be toxic to the organism. An organization's skin is its brand, its culture, and the way it presents itself to the public— in other words, its public image. Let's say an organization was founded to protect a city's animals from harm. That's a strong purpose, but how does that organization appear to the public and the city's officials who have the power to make changes that affect animals? Such an organization could be led by academics and researchers who focus on proving that animals should be spared from pain and suffering. Another organization with this mission could be led by passionate activists who organize massive protests in front of city hall and picket research facilities that experiment on live animals. Each of these organizations would appear quite different to their public and officials. More importantly, their particular public image would help to attract people and opportunities that would benefit them while repelling those that would do them harm. Even though the public image of an organization cannot keep out all pests who would do the organism harm, it acts as an important barrier to many common injuries and ailments.

POLICIES AND PROCEDURES: Policies and procedures are the nervous system because they guide the people of an organization. Without bylaws that spell out the purpose and the roles of leaders, anyone can take charge and use the organization for their personal benefit. Employees without an employee manual develop their own expectations that are usually dashed, causing them to quit, or worse, retaliate. Effective policies and procedures capture the culture of your organization in writing and deflect harmful behavior.

COMMUNICATION: Communication, external and internal, makes up the two most vital structural elements. External communication is like the human respiratory system and internal communication is like the circulatory system. For instance, newsletters and events keep the community involved and inspired as they boost the organization's public image. Internal communication brings life to policies and procedures by supporting a healthy culture and team spirit. Together they keep the breathing and heartbeat steady.

1.2 Summing up the Body Structure Analogy

- BALANCE: energy intake (NUTRITION) and output (EXERCISE);
- PEOPLE: Many varied, actively involved (MUSCLES);
- PURPOSE: A clear, single-sentence mission statement (SKELETON);
- PUBLIC IMAGE: Lots of support in the community (SKIN);
- POLICIES AND PROCEDURES: Concise, effective (NERVOUS SYSTEM);
- EXTERNAL COMMUNICATION: Frequent, well-received (RESPIRATORY SYSTEM); and
- INTERNAL COMMUNICATION: Upbeat, inspiring (CIRCULATORY SYSTEM).

1.3 Appropriate Size

Let's now look at how size affects the health of an organization. Most importantly, there is no best size. The size of your organization should fit its purpose and culture and thus result in a balance between energy consumed (person hours, office infrastructure, administrative supplies, funding, etc.) and energy released in order to achieve that purpose.

If an organization is formed to achieve one project, perhaps to turn a vacant lot into a community garden and disband when it is finished, there is no reason for it ever to be larger than the small group of passionate people, working from their homes, who are focused on this finite goal. Such organizations are similar to temporary project-specific committees. Other organizations that can stay small and remain quite healthy include social clubs and local associations that only seek to bring like-minded people together on a regular schedule, but have no high-impact purpose in mind. I call these "kitchen table organizations" because that's often where meetings take place. There's no need for them to incorporate, though I always recommend that they approve basic bylaws that include the purpose, roles of the leaders, and how those leaders are chosen. This prevents them being taken over by self-serving individuals.

On the other extreme, an organization might be founded to fight an entrenched injustice, much as the ANC was. There is no way the ANC could have crushed apartheid as a kitchen table organization. But is the ANC such a great example of a huge organization? I have my doubts. Now that apartheid has ended, they seem to have lost their focus. This doesn't mean that the ANC never should have become huge. They had to match the size of the colossal injustice they were fighting. In fact, the ANC is a very unusual organization to have spent any of its life as an enormous yet effective organization. Most organizations of its size offer very little benefit in relation to their size.

Questions and concerns about the size of organizations are some of the most common I encounter when coaching. The leaders I advise are usually concerned about how to grow their organization without considering an appropriate size that would meet their needs. During our discussions we often find that a small, agile organization will hasten their particular change better than if they were to grow into one with a large office and many staff.

Imagine two boxers, one featherweight, the other heavyweight—two very different styles. A small boxer can adjust movements and achieve blows that a heavyweight would never try. Of course a featherweight cannot defeat a heavyweight, so work with your team on proper assessment of your most likely opponents. Depending on the mission and its immediate goals, a quick, featherweight organization may be the most likely to succeed.

This boxing image is, unfortunately, the closest I've come to connecting appropriate size to the health and body-structure analogy I use throughout this book. At its birth, an organization has only a few, tentative people holding it together. That's a long way from stepping into any boxing ring. The organization needs to grow out of this fragile state and form a healthy, appropriately sized structure as soon as possible. The closest thing to this tenuous state I could think of within the body analogy was conception, but I realized I'd be wandering right into a sex education analogy—not my comfort zone.

Then there are the oversized organizations. Most of them, simply to survive, do nothing but consume resources and energy from the communities they were supposed to serve. Their gluttony is so great I considered using cancer as an analogy. But cancer consumes only the body of its victim, not those around it. While cancer torments the victim's loved ones, it does not consume their bodies. I could have explored exotic, disgusting diseases that do consume people in the vicinity of their victims, but I'm sure that neither you nor I would have much enjoyed that.

1.4 Star Analogy: Nebulous, Balanced, or Red Giant

Thus I must temporarily shift into a different analogy to

help you assess the appropriate size of your organization, not just today, but well into its future. I'm going to use stars. Please bear with me.

A man with a kind voice once phoned to ask the size of organizations he should contribute to. He had called One Street and had referred to bicycle initiatives, but I took his question in a broad context. I nearly blurted out, "Small, at the local level," but caught myself to consider my answer more carefully.

That's when I remembered a lesson on the lives of stars from when I was in elementary school. What had fascinated me in that lesson, even as a child, was that not all stars are flaming balls of energy that spend their days warming planets as our sun does. Some are new and struggling. Others are old and actually suck energy from space.

New organizations are much like new stars; just dust and gas swirling around, but drawn together by a powerful force. As a child, I was sorry to learn that many new stars never become true stars because the force is not great enough to bring them together or other forces pull them apart. If I had blurted out, "Small, at the local level," as my answer to this man, it would have included these vulnerable organizations and may not have been good advice.

I described this elementary school lesson and noted that his contribution could very well be the force that stabilizes a small organization, but pointed out the risk that it could dissolve anyway. Still, the potential of making a much greater impact with his contribution, big risk vs. big payoff, could be enticing.

Next I described stars like our sun and the appropriately sized organizations they match. These have found a balance between the force that pulled them together, which still pulls inward, and the energy they give out to benefit the world around them. Their size is just right—not so big that the inward force consumes them and not so small that they have little energy to offer. I tried to describe to this man what such an organization might look like—the confidence of its leaders, its excellent reputation, and most of all an undertone of fun in everything the leaders do and say. Determining large or small was not important. Instead, I urged the man to look for signs of appropriate size—a balance of healthy structure and energy output that align with the organization's mission. A contribution to such an organization would very likely make a positive impact.

But then there were the red giants. These were stars that no longer had energy to offer. They had run out of material with which to create energy and had begun to consume themselves. As they turned inward, they created a hard shell that expanded as the internal consumption devoured the star. Eventually the shell stretched so thin that it pulled apart, leaving the vacuum of internal focus swirling into a black hole, desperately grabbing at anything that came within reach.

There is indeed a desperation about red giant organizations. They seem to believe that as long as everyone who works for them is doing something, they're okay. Yet if you ask people outside the organization what it has done to benefit its target community, no one can say. Much like red giant stars, these organizations usually create hard, exclusive shells that prevent people from getting involved or learning much about them. Instead, they focus inward using exclusive jargon to create extravagant materials that justify their existence. And just like red giant stars, these massive, expanding organizations eventually run out of internal energy, their hard outer shells collapse and, in their desperation, they grab at other organizations, stealing credit for the others' work. I told this man that donating to such an organization would be like throwing his money into a black hole.

I never like to encounter a red giant organization. I can't help them because they aren't looking for help. In fact, they likely will never recognize the harm they are doing by consuming energy that could have gone instead to effective, appropriately sized organizations. Even worse, because they are large, they can withstand and absorb ailments, unlike smaller organizations. Their leadership team could be ripping themselves to shreds or in full corruption, but their inertia keeps them barreling along the same destructive path. Recently, we witnessed the final stage of this as countless financial institutions finally ground to a halt after many years of despicable consumption when even their leaders proudly proclaimed they were too big to fail.

One of the worst types of harm I've witnessed from red giants is when they persuade otherwise healthy organizations to behave the way they do. I have encountered too many appropriately sized organizations that have everything going for them—a strong and clear purpose, enthusiastic leaders, lots of support from their community—and yet choose to follow the actions of red giant organizations. They ignore their core supporters to spend their time courting huge foundations that likely will never give them the time of day. They trample smaller organizations in order to take credit for work they did not do. They reach beyond their purpose and community to grab at any opportunity for money or power.

Consider whether your organization has found a healthy balance between inward pull and contributing outward energy to your target community. Is all the energy being spent on meetings and team support or, at the other extreme, infighting? Do you use jargon that excludes new people? These could be signs that you are moving into the red giant danger zone. Are all of you providing services to your community without attending to the health of your organization? This could hold you in that nebulous, new-star form that remains vulnerable to malicious forces.

I realize that this star analogy could seem to contradict the organism analogy this book is based on, but it really doesn't. If you set aside the fact that stars are not living organisms, the rest of their makeup fits with organizations quite nicely, especially the way they are formed and whether or not they provide beneficial energy. One other important difference is that stars cannot bring in new material with which to create beneficial energy, but organizations can, and must. In other words, all stars of significance eventually will become red giants, but organizations have the choice not to.

Health is easy to identify. We are attracted to it and seek simple ways to achieve it. By now you should have several healthy organizations in mind; perhaps a charter school, a dog owners' club, a neighborhood watch group, or a gang intervention organization. Their boards are strong and working as a team with the executive director. Each executive director is confident and comfortable in his or her position. Appropriate candidates for the board are regularly invited to take part in activities and learn about the organization before being invited to serve. The organization is following a plan that aligns with its mission. Start a list of your favorite healthy organizations so you can refer to them as you work through this book and bring your organization back to health. Consider how they present themselves and attract great people to help their efforts. Reach out to them and note how they communicate with you. Use them as your models for your own organization.

Ailments are a different story. Our first reaction is to deny they exist. That cough is nothing. That pain will go away. Soon they become part of us, something we work around. As they get worse, we can justify putting off treatment because there are so many immediate tasks to take care of. When they finally overwhelm us and we are forced to take action, we often waste far too much time and money treating for the wrong ailment. That is why proper diagnosis is so very important.

In the next chapter we'll look at diagnosis so that you can discover exactly what is compromising the health of your organization.

Chapter 2
Diagnosis

Proper diagnosis is the first and most critical step toward curing an organization's ailments. Your organization is ailing if it is no longer able to focus its energy on its mission. Beyond that, you will have to identify the ailments and determine whether you are facing a crisis, thus requiring immediate first aid, or whether you have the luxury of a more relaxed response. Compare traumatic injuries and sudden illnesses with diseases that settle in over time. The former can be caused by the latter, but not always. And the latter can and should be treated before it reaches a crisis level. As you read on about the worst danger signs, be sure to take note of each one even if it does not fit your current situation. Simply knowing these danger signs can help you in the future to identify potential threats before they become a problem.

I will start this chapter with the first aid diagnosis to help you determine if you are facing a crisis. Discovering that your organization is in danger can be terrifying. We fear things we do not understand. Analyzing and learning about the common causes of these unsettling events are the first steps toward stabilizing your organization. What once was nightmarish will become a tangible problem that you can solve.

The rest of this chapter will help you diagnose less dangerous concerns including those that may have led to a crisis. Most often, these are isolated ailments that can be cured easily. Even emergencies that require immediate attention often signify underlying ailments that need more comprehensive treatment. Study these seemingly simple diagnoses with an eye toward preventing more serious difficulties in the future.

2.1 Diagnosing Life-Threatening Crises

All life-threatening crises result in communication breakdowns, both external and internal. During a crisis, leaders of organizations will stop sending news and updates to their community and will no longer update their website. Internally, meetings will become either brutal or silent if they happen at all. Internal reports and updates become rarities. Staff, volunteers, and members will be left with only hearsay and gossip as they try to understand what is going on. If you are seeing any such symptoms, you are likely facing an urgent situation.

Some organization disasters can occur within weeks, obliterating the organization before most in the community realize there was a problem. This is why immediate action is needed if you suspect this level of danger. Much like sudden injuries and illnesses, the causes of sudden organization emergencies can often be traced back to deep, systemic problems within the framework of the organization. This is particularly so for external and internal communication, or as I explained, the respiratory and circulatory systems of your organization.

Imagine the respiratory system as the communications you send to people outside of your organization—press releases, e-newsletters, blog posts, funder reports, and in-person gatherings—that inform them of your latest accomplishments. Such communications can also be ongoing—web page updates, new brochures, links from partner websites, social media posts—that provide an overview of your organization and the work you are currently doing. When these stop, your organization has stopped breathing.

Now imagine the circulatory system as your internal communication such as reports to the board, treasurer's reports, and meeting minutes. This circulatory system also includes informal communication, that is, how all of you communicate with each other. In fact, informal communications are often more accurate for diagnosing a circulatory emergency because formal reports can easily leave out concerns. When internal communication stops or becomes sporadic, your organization is having a heart attack.

If you have ever taken a first aid course, you will likely remember ABC: A = airway, B = breathing, C = circulation (recently changed to CAB to prioritize circulation, but for this book I will stick to ABC). When you come upon someone who may need first aid, you start by determining if their airway is open, then if they are breathing and have a good pulse. Circulation also includes bleeding and determining whether the patient is losing enough blood to warrant immediate treatment. From this simple assessment a first aid responder can determine the steps they must take to save the person's life. Keep your organization assessment similarly simple.

Before attempting first aid, a well-trained responder will first call for assistance. Next, the responder will assess and stabilize the surrounding environment. What caused the injury? If this is a stabbing, is the assailant still in the area? If the victim fell, are they now in a stable position or could you and the victim fall farther? If the victim was in a car crash or house fire, are they far enough away from potential explosions or similar threats?

For an organization facing a life-threatening emergency, follow similar steps and look for comparable danger signs. Who is causing the harm? Who is helping or are you the only one addressing this concern? Who is complacent but should be helping? Who else can help? Is there something in the environment that is causing the emergency? Scan the whole picture before taking action.

By regarding external communication as the airway and breathing, you will know that immediate action is necessary when they are compromised. Find out why your latest newsletter was not sent. Ask when the last press release went out. Check the dates of the last website updates. An even greater concern is when such communications are harming the organization. These could be slanderous comments made to people outside of the organization or worse, to officials and the media. They could also be inappropriate messages sent out under the banner of the organization by a well-meaning member of your team. No matter the intent, the damage can cut deep into your organization's reputation and require years to repair. Take note of every such communication and who was responsible.

By regarding internal communication as circulation you will better recognize concerns. Much like the pulse of your organization, either absent or erratic communication signals danger. Observe interactions within your organization. How are people communicating with each other and during meetings? Has someone been fired or removed without cause? Are there particular individuals who seem to be causing the trouble? Are there policies in place that offer guidance for stopping this behavior? Are leaders leaving without reason? Are potential new leaders turning down your invitations to serve?

Funding crises align with bleeding and so are also communication (circulation) emergencies. A bit of blood from a nasty cut should not distract the first aid responder from taking care of the airway and regaining circulation. But if the victim is breathing and gushing blood, that bleeding must be stopped. When responding to an organization in crisis, don't be distracted by minor financial troubles, but you will need to take immediate action for severe financial concerns. Theft and misuse of money are obvious. However, dangers are often not so obvious. For instance, many financial disasters occur because of total reliance on a single source of funding that suddenly stopped. Another example is when funding is accepted for a program or project that does not align with the organization's mission. For now, take note of shortfalls and improper earmarks, how they may have occurred and who is responsible.

Sometimes a crisis can be caused by external forces. These

often come from leaders of other organizations who feel threatened by yours. For instance, I have often coached leaders through attacks by former leaders of a long-dead organization that once had a similar mission. They seem to take offense that anyone would build a similar organization. I refer to these as "zombie attacks." A comparable sort of attack can come from leaders of another organization who take credit for your work. If you are facing an external attack, take note of the individuals who are responsible and their inappropriate communications.

As you assess your situation and note important details, don't let a lot of screaming bother you. If people are shouting or complaining or demanding discussion, you are likely facing an ailment, but not a crisis. Just as in a medical emergency, screaming is a relief. It means the victim's airway is open and they are breathing just fine. The quiet victims are the scariest. This is often the case with organizations as well. For instance, if your executive director is threatening to quit, immediate treatment is necessary, but at least they are communicating. If your executive director has vanished, you are likely facing a full-blown crisis.

Below is the first of several diagnosis checklists you will find in this chapter. Check every box that applies to your situation.

You are likely facing a life-threatening crisis if:

- ☐ External communication has stopped.
- ☐ External communications are harming the organization, either misleading or slanderous.
- ☐ Leaders or employees are badmouthing or otherwise harming the organization and current policies offer no guidance for stopping this behavior.
- ☐ Factions within the leadership are fully engaged in conflict or, worse, avoiding each other.
- ☐ The executive director has been fired without cause or similar brutality has been committed on other individuals.
- ☐ Leaders are avoiding meetings and work.

- ☐ Leaders have left and potential new leaders are repelled.
- ☐ Staff, members, and volunteers have no idea what is going on.
- ☐ Leaders of another organization are taking credit for or slandering your work.
- ☐ Leaders of a long-dead organization are trying to stop your work and their previous failures are being projected onto your organizations.
- ☐ You relied on a single source of funding and that funding did not come through.
- ☐ Significant funding has been stolen or misused.
- ☐ Significant funding is earmarked for activities that have nothing to do with the organization's mission.
- ☐ A significant loan cannot be repaid or renegotiated.

You'll read more about assessing your crisis prior to treatment in the following chapters. For now, be sure to check all boxes above that pertain to what you have found so you will know whether or not you are facing a crisis. Each item you check in this and the following checklists will be fully covered later.

2.2 Diagnosing Less-Threatening Ailments

Now we will work on diagnosing ailments that, on their own, rarely threaten the life of an organization. Still, just as with any ailment, if they are left untreated they can advance into a life-threatening form. With this in mind, take their treatment seriously. Also, stay alert for any of the danger signs noted earlier in this chapter because a minor injury or illness can suddenly escalate into a crisis without warning. This can be through rapid deterioration of the victim, unrecognized symptoms of more serious problems, or the surrounding environment that originally caused the problem. Organization emergencies are always revealed through communication problems so keep a careful eye on all communications as you and your team diagnose your particular ailments.

To help you discover what is ailing your organization, I have divided most of the rest of this chapter into these five diagnostic categories, each with their own checklist of symptoms:

2.3 Diagnosing People Ailments
2.4 Diagnosing Purpose (Mission) Ailments
2.5 Diagnosing Public Image Ailments
2.6 Diagnosing Policy and Procedure Ailments
2.7 Diagnosing Communication Ailments

Before we get started, I realize that some readers will not be leaders of the organization they are trying to help. This makes diagnosis and assistance more difficult because you have little access to vital information and no power to make changes, but it's certainly not impossible. Diagnosing a crisis should be straightforward because you can easily identify inappropriate or missing communications, but uncovering what caused an ailment is usually more complex. First you will have to gain the trust of the leaders and find a way to begin an honest discussion. If you have funded the organization, they will be inclined to give you a rosy picture in order to secure more funding from you. Find a way past this or you will not get anywhere. If you are simply someone who values the organization, but has not yet stepped up to help lead it, be honest with your intentions and thoroughly explain why you are so eager to help. Leaders of struggling organizations are often suspicious of people's intentions because people are likely the cause of their struggles.

As an outsider you will need to learn all the intricacies that led to the problem in order to do a good job of diagnosis. I go through this every time a troubled leader calls me for help at One Street. Always ask the leaders *why* they did something and what their original intentions were, if they don't offer such details. By asking these questions, you will prompt them to reveal how well they are (or aren't) working together. Also, by not jumping to your own conclusion about their actions, you will show them that you respect their leadership role. The more questions you ask, the more they can explain. Remember, you cannot offer appropriate assistance until the ailment is correctly diagnosed. At this stage, let them do most of the talking. Take ample notes. Don't expect to remember the details of your discussion if you don't write them down. Anxious leaders often blurt out important details in random order. By referring to your notes, you can help center their thoughts and ask them to fill in gaps so you can formulate a diagnosis together.

As we prepare to look at each diagnostic category, keep in mind that they are meant to be synchronized in order to achieve health. Without a clear purpose, people in organizations move about erratically or stop moving all together. Without appropriate policies and procedures, these same people can turn against the organization and do it harm. If the public image is disturbing, no new people will come to the organization and officials will dismiss its proposals. An organization cannot be healthy without all of these systems intact and working together.

Now, let's dig into each.

2.3 Diagnosing People Ailments

An organization's people are like its muscles. In order to work toward its mission, they must know their roles and work together, never against each other. This includes proud leaders who are taking responsibility for the entire organization, looking at it as a whole and making decisions in its best interest. These are usually the board members and executive director all working together. I will refer to the top staff position as executive director throughout this book, though they can also be called the CEO or president, if the president is the top staff position.

Without leaders, no one else in the organization—employees, specialists, experts, volunteers—will know what they should be doing. I often encounter young organizations that were formed without leaders. The idea is that everyone should have a chance to make decisions for the organization. The problem is that most people are not leaders and would much prefer to spend their time offering their particular skills, not having to look at and decide for the entire organization. Another problem is that if everyone is responsible, no one is responsible. Decisions won't be made when needed and the organization can easily spiral into crisis. A similar dynamic can occur when more than twelve board members are allowed. There's something about the number twelve that ensures all leaders remain actively involved, as long as they are appropriate leaders. With more than twelve on a board, even good leaders will tend to fade away believing that someone else will take care of their duties. Of course there are exceptions to this tendency, but they occur because of extraordinary individuals. I recommend keeping common tendencies in mind when making such policy decisions. The best place to designate your maximum number of board members is in your organization's bylaws, discussed later.

Other policies and procedures that can lead to people ailments include allowing committees of the board to make decisions for the entire organization (a big no-no) and executive director agreements that set this person out as inferior to the board.

If an organization has a damaged reputation or is simply not well known, the current leaders will have a very difficult time attracting new leaders to join them. This can result in burnout of the current leaders and a downward spiral into crisis. The concept of "board recruitment" only causes frustration when not accompanied by activities, fun events, and a welcoming atmosphere that engages many people of all types and abilities. By engaging lots of people all the time, you will find among them those few with the rare talents of leaders. When you find potential leaders this way, they will already understand and support the purpose of your organization. This avoids many all-too-common ailments and crises caused by inappropriate people invited to serve as board members for organizations they care little about. Consider the criteria you and your team use for board members.

People are always central to life-threatening crises. At this point, we are looking at less frightening situations such as misunderstandings, confusion over roles, and missed expectations. Even so, any ailment caused by people can easily escalate into an emergency. People perceive their own realities that often can be quite different from the realities of others. So diagnosing ailments caused by people can be quite complicated because some, including the perpetrators, may not even know there is a problem.

People ailments usually lead to factions. Either one leader or employee begins acting on their own or groups split and begin taking separate, contrary actions. Differentiate between contrary views, which should always be encouraged, and truly harmful actions that are purposely counter to the organization's direction. If these actions are significant and causing harm, and there are no policies in place to offer guidance, you are in the midst of a crisis. Also, if you believe you are a victim of misbehavior by other people in your organization, this is a crisis. In these situations a victim cannot defend themselves, so even the slightest ailment escalates immediately to an emergency. Make sure you checked the appropriate boxes in the first part of this chapter.

Even when the results of factions and misbehaviors are minor, they can easily lead to an emergency, so immediate treatment is necessary. Don't let this continue.

Whether you are one of the organization's leaders or someone on the outside eager to help, you need to narrow down where the people problems are occurring. Check any boxes below that apply:

- ☐ A lone leader or employee is taking independent action or overriding others.
- ☐ Separate groups have formed within the organization and are working against each other.
- ☐ Confusion over roles has led to redundancies, micromanaging, and tasks left undone.
- ☐ The number of board members has dropped well below the number allowed.

☐ No new people have joined the board in more than two years.

☐ The number of board members allowed is more than twelve.

☐ People who care nothing about the organization or show no leadership skills have been invited to serve on the board.

☐ Committees of the board (often an "executive committee") and factions are allowed to make decisions for the entire organization.

☐ Board members are elected without any prior involvement with the organization.

☐ The executive director has a time-limited agreement.

☐ The executive director is considered a contractor.

☐ The executive director's salary is well below the market rate.

☐ A lower staff position has been filled before hiring an executive director.

2.4 Diagnosing Purpose (Mission) Ailments

The overarching diagnosis of any ailment (crisis level or not) is that the organization cannot focus its energy on its mission. One possible cause of this is that the purpose, and the mission statement that describes it, is flawed. An organization's purpose is like its skeleton. It reaches to every extremity and is the framework upon which everything else connects. If the purpose itself is defective, this can explain why no one can put their energy toward it.

A vague mission statement can appear to be quite adequate as long as everything is going smoothly. But when strange problems continue to stop your work, when your fellow leaders argue over what the organization should be doing, stop working altogether, or waste their time on useless tasks, you will want to take a much closer look at your mission statement.

I often discover vague mission statements at the center of

troubles plaguing bicycle organizations. Mission statements like: "More people bicycling" or "Safe streets for all" seem wonderfully concise at first glance. Then imagine you are a new leader coming into the organization ready to help. What is the organization supposed to be doing? Where does it work? Is it local, national, or international? How can you distinguish it from other bicycle organizations with similar mission statements?

Let's try a better version: "To influence policy and legislation so that all streets in Brazil are safe and inviting for even the most novice bicyclist." Now, if you are a new leader for *this* organization you will know that your work is confined to Brazil, that you are a national lobbying organization, and that local programs like bike rides and bicycle education classes are not appropriate. Even an initiative to allow bikes on trains would be outside this mission. The organization could support the work of organizations leading such programs, but they could not make them primary programs of theirs. Such a clear mission does a much better job.

Another common purpose ailment involves complex mission statements longer than one sentence. I have seen far too many multi-sentence and even page-length mission statements that include everything from the history of the organization to the founders' childhood memories. Such embellishments do nothing but confuse. A mission statement should fit into one concise sentence with each word doing significant work to explain exactly what the organization was founded to accomplish. There are more appropriate places to put all the embellishments, which I will discuss later.

The key to diagnosing purpose ailments is knowing what you are supposed to be doing. A healthy organization cannot do everything well. Your mission statement needs to define and differentiate the work you expect to do. This is critical. If you don't know what you are supposed to be doing, how will you know whether or not you're doing it?

If you are an outsider, you will have to learn the necessary information from one or more of the leaders. Start by asking what the purpose of the organization is rather than the mission. By asking about the purpose you will allow them to adlib while still relaying the basic information you need. Asking what the mission is might imply that you are testing them to see if they know their mission statement by heart. However, if the leader does state the mission statement, this is a very good sign. If not, you can ask them to point you to their mission statement on their website or email it to you.

Check any boxes below that apply:
- ☐ The mission statement is presented differently in various materials.
- ☐ The mission statement is too vague or complex for most people to remember.
- ☐ The mission statement does not match the level of significance and impact or the culture intended by the founders and its current leaders.
- ☐ The organization's purpose is redundant to other organizations in the area.

2.5 Diagnosing Public Image Ailments

An organization's public image is like its skin. It develops through a combination of forces, some controlled by its leaders, others not. The more control the leaders have the better because the other forces generally revolve around gossip and misinformation. If you suspect public image ailments, you will have to rely on people outside of the organization to give you the necessary details. What matters most about these ailments has little to do with how the people within the organization feel about it. However, if you have also suspected that people on your team have been slandering and badmouthing the organization, you may be looking at a combination of people and public image ailments. If there are no policies in place that offer guidance for dealing with people behaving this way, you are facing a crisis.

Even if you have policies in place and have managed to

quiet or let go the people doing the badmouthing, the leaders will have quite a bit of work to do repairing the public image.

A good public image correctly captures the organization's mission as well as the ideals and culture intended by its leaders. Is it radical or academic? Is it a place to hang out or a high-level think tank? Does it gently guide policy makers or force them to take action? Every one of these options is appropriate, but if the public image differs from the one intended by the leaders, there's an ailment that needs to be remedied.

You can discover a damaged public image several ways. Perhaps the most disturbing is finding misinformation published in mainstream media. But misinformation delivered from one person who heard it from another can be just as dangerous because such rumors can often spread faster and farther than media blurbs. If you only suspect such rumors, but haven't heard them yourself, you will need to talk with people you trust in your community and confirm this problem before making the mistake of responding to rumors that do not exist.

Remember, people flock to a healthy organization. If this is not happening, there's a very good chance its public image is scaring them away.

Check any boxes below that apply:
- ☐ Misinformation about the organization is spreading throughout its community.
- ☐ The organization's website, materials, and brand— name, logo, colors, and slogan—do not align with its intended image.

2.6 Diagnosing Policy and Procedure Ailments
By imagining policies and procedures as an organization's nervous system we will grant their ailments an appropriate level of urgency. Just as with our nervous system, we do not want such ailments to take hold and compromise our activities. Creating policies and procedures can seem terribly mundane and boring, especially when everything is going great and everyone is getting

along. Some policies are safety devices, often only put into service when trouble strikes and thus easily put off. Others, like the annual work plan/budget, bookkeeping system, and donor care, influence daily procedures. Without these, bad behaviors can easily take hold. More importantly, they cannot be created in the midst of crisis.

Carrying out appropriate policies and procedures should be balanced with beneficial activities. For instance, if leaders focus entirely on winning new bikeways and spend no time attracting members or raising funds to pay staff, they may win a few bikeways, but will burn out, leaving only disappointed constituents when they step away. On the other extreme, if leaders spend all their time inputting financial data, upgrading software, and attending nonprofit seminars, they will have nothing to show for their work and no one will even recognize the organization.

The number of programs, projects and campaigns an organization takes on can also affect its performance. I always recommend no more than three, all clearly defined and advancing toward the organization's mission. Any fewer and you run the risk of being identified with a single program. Any more and you will spread your resources too thin, confusing your team and community as to what you are supposed to be doing. This applies no matter the size of the organization. Small organizations need three small programs or projects underway, large should take on larger ones. Even if you have several activities, campaigns, and initiatives going on, try to fit them into just three program categories. If they do not fit into three, your organization is likely taking on too many and too varied activities. Ongoing administrative activities like partner development, fundraising, and office support, while necessary for an organization's success, do not count as programs because they do not directly advance the organization's mission.

Leaders abide by policies and procedures not because they are forced to, but because they helped create them or upgrade them to fit the healthy operations of their organization. Leaders understand that some policies are there only as a last-resort safety net in an emergency. In healthy organizations, leaders adhere to their culture of kindness and respect for each other without having to refer to their policies. Leaders bring their policies to life through their ongoing actions and behaviors.

Check any boxes below that apply (several are repeated from People Ailments as they apply to both):

- ☐ Meetings are not productive.
- ☐ There are no bylaws, or existing bylaws have gaps or inappropriate language.
- ☐ Confusion over roles has led to redundancies, micromanaging, and tasks left undone.
- ☐ The number of board members allowed is more than twelve.
- ☐ The board is member-elected without safeguards to prevent takeover.
- ☐ Committees of the board (often an "executive committee") and factions are allowed to make decisions for the entire organization.
- ☐ Board members are elected without any prior involvement with the organization.
- ☐ No annual work plan/budget has been developed and passed by the board.
- ☐ There are fewer than three programs underway at all times; none inspire new helpers.
- ☐ Too many programs and campaigns are taken on.
- ☐ No policy regulates external communication or the use of the organization's brand (name, logo, slogan, colors, fonts, etc.).
- ☐ The executive director has a time-limited agreement.
- ☐ The executive director is considered a contractor.
- ☐ The executive director's salary is well below the market rate.
- ☐ There is no employee manual that contains general expectations of employees.

☐ Members, donors, and potential volunteers have no easy way to take part in activities.

☐ Members, donors, and volunteers are often not thanked for their contribution and are rarely updated on the progress of the programs they care about.

☐ Operations systems are not up to current standards and the office environment is causing poor morale.

☐ Bookkeeping goes undone.

☐ Taxes have not been filed on schedule.

2.7 Diagnosing Communication Ailments

External and internal communications, like the respiratory and circulatory systems, are supposed to be constant and provide ongoing benefits, never harm. If this is not the case for you and your team, you will have noted already that a crisis is in full swing.

However, communication disorders do not always signal a crisis. For instance, when organization successes are not promoted and pass without notice, they fail to provide any benefit to the long-term health of the organization.

Leaders of healthy organizations are proud to parade their accomplishments. They look for every opportunity to demonstrate their organization's good work through eye-catching materials and presentations. Every time their organization achieves something, they distribute a press release to every media channel that has even the remotest connection to their work and region. They keep their website updated with all of these news items. They send out exciting e-newsletters each month to everyone who has ever connected with their organization. All of these important contacts are gathered regularly and kept up-to-date. And all of these communications include the same logo and colors to brand the organization in the minds of their constituents.

Without such a comprehensive promotion system and culture for ongoing communication to supporters and potential supporters, an organization will fade away. Also, scattered promotions that include different logos, colors, and slogans will diminish the effectiveness of each communication because viewers will not know they are related.

Be confident in all of your external communication, but don't confuse confidence with deception. Report on true accomplishments and announce upcoming plans that were approved by the board and soon to be underway. Never promise products, services, or achievements that are not absolutely guaranteed. Failed promises always undermine an organization's reputation.

Be honest in all of your external communication, but leave out the uninteresting details. I like to refer to such details as "sausage making." Your fans only want to see the end result and don't need to be dragged through the gory details of how you got there. I recently unsubscribed from an e-newsletter for a publishing organization I belong to because they were sending out weekly updates on each step they were taking to rebuild their board. Not only was I disturbed by their excruciating process, I simply didn't want to read about it. As a member, I want information on publishing, not their sausage making.

Another form of sausage making occurs when young organizations present themselves as young. "We are a new organization tackling hunger in (city)." The tackling hunger part is great, but do people really want to risk wasting their time or money with an organization that considers itself new? Is this information important? No, it's sausage making. Certainly post your founding year, perhaps on a web page about the organization and in the history section of proposals, but don't make "new" or "young" part of your main description. Potential helpers can decide for themselves what they consider to be new or young.

As you can see, external communications have a tight connection with the public image of the organization, but they are not the same. Just because you send out a dazzling e-newsletter does not mean everyone will read or believe it. There are many other factors involved in an organization's public image, including hearsay, rumors, and gossip. External communications are still important. Without them, the public will have to rely entirely on the rumor mill.

Internal communications are the critical flow of information between people within the organization. Much like the circulatory system, they carry nutrients to vital parts and transport waste out. Without healthy internal communication, outdated or false information (waste) builds up and can create factions and rogues. People in organizations need a constant flow of up-to-date information. Healthy internal communication takes place in frequent, productive meetings as well as through concise updates whenever needed. Don't confuse this with information overflow, which amounts to sausage making. For instance, program employees do not need to witness the budgeting process, but they do need to see the final budget.

Funding ailments are in the communication category because they rely on both external and internal communication. Donors contribute and customers return because they receive positive updates about your organization. Internally, your team should develop a reasonable budget along with a work plan that includes many varied sources of funding. Such teamwork depends on healthy internal communication.

Funding shortfalls can escalate to the crisis level much like bleeding during a medical emergency. Minor funding ailments, as with minor wounds, can eventually lead to major losses if not treated. Ensure there are enough varied funding sources to withstand the unpleasant news that one has fallen short. Most should rely on contributions from many individuals such as membership dues, sales of products, fundraising events, crowd fundraising, fees for service, and the like. Only a few should be large contributions from a single source such as grants and government contracts, and these should never dominate your budget. Funding mechanisms that tap many individuals are under your control and they never vanish overnight as single sources tend to do.

Tapping funding from many individuals may seem like a

lot of work compared to receiving one grant to cover expenses, but it will be worth it in the long run. That is because it also brings people to your organization. You need to reach out for new members and renewals. You have to sell your products. Even if you do a mediocre job, you'll attract some people and money. In contrast, a grant is out of your hands. You can submit an award-winning proposal, but the grant committee can still turn it down. In response, you and your team can ramp up your fundraising efforts with individuals to cover the loss, that is, if you have such funding mechanisms in place.

This underscores why you should never include a particular grant as income in a budget until it is in the organization's bank account. It's okay to include a general "grants" line item in your budget as long as you realize that only ten percent of flawless grant proposals are ever funded. A grants line item assumes the submission of at least ten exquisite proposals sent to perfectly matched funders in order to secure any funding at all.

Check any boxes below that apply:

☐ Months have passed without external communication.
☐ The organization's website is outdated.
☐ There is no consistency in branding (logo, colors, and slogan).
☐ Promises made in previous communications have failed.
☐ The organization took credit for another organization's work.
☐ Important news is buried in uninteresting information.
☐ Board meetings are too infrequent or regularly postponed and canceled.
☐ Board members do not receive pertinent reports before meetings.
☐ Regular meetings last for more than one hour and are dominated by information that could have been sent in report form prior to the meeting.
☐ Internal communication is inconsistent and infrequent.

- [ ] Employees and volunteers rely on hearsay to determine what is happening.
- [ ] Employees and volunteers sit idly or are uncertain what to do.
- [ ] Income projections in the work plan/budget were not met.
- [ ] No annual work plan/budget.
- [ ] Too few sources of income and not enough from individuals.

2.8 Final Thoughts on Diagnosis

On rare occasions, after a thorough diagnosis, disbanding the organization becomes the only option. This can involve a lone leader taking over the organization. If you and your whole team decide that such a leader should be granted full control over the organization, then the best remedy is to change the structure to a for-profit sole proprietorship and disband the board. This leader will then become the sole proprietor, owner/operator and have all the freedom he or she needs to pursue their dreams.

Occasionally an organization will have the fatal flaw that it was founded only to make money or gain power from a cause the leaders care nothing about. This flaw is so noxious there is no remedy. I have encountered such organizations most often in areas of the world that recently faced a well-publicized disaster or are famously impoverished. Because of all the media attention, some people can be tempted to form a nonprofit for the sole purpose of collecting donations or manipulating other people. If the organization you are trying to help exhibits similar traits, ask all the leaders to take an honest look at their intentions. To continue such a charade is not only harmful to the cause they have hijacked, it is illegal. Disbanding is the only responsible choice.

If you have found blatant misuse of funds or misuse of the organization by its leaders, your country should have laws in place to deal with this situation. Contact the appropriate authorities, but not until you have thoroughly investigated the situation, spoken directly with the organization's leaders, and are convinced of illegal activity.

Now that you have worked through the diagnosis, read on to learn how to respond to common organization crises. Remedies for less-threatening ailments will follow after that.

Chapter 3
Understanding Causes of Crises

Once you have diagnosed a crisis in your organization, you need to respond quickly. I will cover remedies for ailments in later chapters because crises need to be brought under control first.

If your organization is in peril, I first want to offer my heartfelt sympathy. I know how horrifying these situations can be, especially for a leader who cares deeply for their organization. Try to breathe as calmly as you can. Take the time to read this and the next chapter before attempting the first aid processes that follow. This background and insight will help to calm you.

Most nonprofits and social enterprises are founded with purposes important to our world. I think we owe it to them to offer a hand when they're down. We can look to the medical response system as a model and as we shift from accepting the demise of organizations to fighting for their recovery, a specialized response system for organizations may one day evolve.

The first organized effort to respond to medical emergencies began with the founding of the Red Cross in 1863. Until then, most people who entered a hospital expected to die, never mind those who had no way of reaching a hospital. It wasn't until the 1960s, when the Emergency Medical Services (EMS) standards were developed, that "victims" became "patients" expected to pull through.

To reach a similar standard, we must first recognize the value of existing organizations. Those visionaries in the late 1800s realized that suffering people had more to offer this world, that to create a standardized medical response system that saved even a few would be worth the tremendous effort. While responding to a tragically wounded organization may seem like a lot of trouble, the effort will pay back many times. If you've read this far, there's a good chance your organization is worth saving.

3.1 Cultures of Brutality

People are always central to any organization crisis. People will also be central to your response. Those central to the crisis are likely on your leadership team. Most nonprofit board members took on the role believing their service would cause positive change. But nonprofit resources usually offer only these responsibilities for board members:

- Hire and oversee the executive director,
- Ensure legal and financial compliance, and
- Fire the executive director.

This reveals an unacceptable correlation between nonprofit and for-profit corporate board duties. The original corporations—even back to the first companies in ancient Rome, ancient India, and medieval Europe—were assumed to be created for the public good. The reason for creating a corporation was to ensure that it outlasted its founders in order to continue its beneficial work. So there was no distinction made between for-profit and nonprofit.

It wasn't until the colonial expansion in the 1600s that lawmakers began to rein in common corporate abuses, most of them financial. Here is where the split begins with the passing of the Statute of Charitable Uses Act of 1601 England. While this law, still referred to today, spent much of its wording on defining charities, its legal teeth focused entirely on the use of funds. By defining charities only through use of funds without recognizing their special needs, this act and the laws that followed it have intensified the problem of low expectations for nonprofits. Even social enterprise organizations suffer from this copy-paste mess.

After this split, for-profit corporations were no longer expected to benefit society. They only need to make money and report detailed financials to shareholders. Nonprofits were then left with the task of benefitting society, but were not required to do so. Because nonprofit boards answer to no one and their reporting requirements remain financial only, for-profit models seem appropriate to many board members. A look at other organization types shows how inappropriate this actually is.

Consider wilderness expeditions, construction crews, and sports teams. These are all types of organizations. A football team would never fire its starting quarterback without cause and then expect him to start each game for the next six months. Would this be a good way to treat the lead climber of a mountain expedition? What about the guy responsible for setting up the scaffolding? And yet this is a common, copy-paste clause in executive director agreements. Here's a classic example, from a national association of nonprofits:

> *Cancellation by the Association without Cause*. The Association may cancel this Agreement for any other reason, which need not be disclosed to the Executive, by giving the Executive written notice of the cancellation and paying full compensation to the Executive during the notice period; at its sole discretion, the Association will determine whether to require that the Executive perform the Executive's duties for the Association during that notice period; the length of that notice period is subject to a minimum of 6 months and a maximum of 12 months, which period may extend beyond the then-current annual term of this Agreement and the Agreement will automatically be extended through that notice period only. Full benefits will be provided to the Executive during this notice period.

Such agreements place the executive in the realm of office

machinery and cause him or her to withdraw from and fear their boards. Cancellation-without-cause, sometimes called removal-without-cause, sections are common in for-profit corporate agreements; they are the model source. This is another example of nonprofits and social enterprises avoiding the difficult work of creating appropriate policies that match their intended culture.

I am not suggesting that once an executive director is hired they should be kept on indefinitely no matter what they do. Later I will discuss proper and respectful methods of removal for any leader, executive director or board member, who is proven to be causing harm to the organization; in other words removal-*with*-cause.

Combine cruel policy language with volunteer boards who unplug because all they ever do is discuss boring legal and financial procedures and we've got an explosive mix. Too many news stories outline the resulting emergencies—executive directors falsifying financial reports, executive committees changing entire organization structures on a whim, rapid-fire turnover that extinguishes all trust in the organization. And yet, organizations and consultants who present themselves as resources for nonprofits continue to spew out copy after copy of cut-and-paste policies that further insulate board members from their initial intentions to do good.

As you assess the threats to your own organization, look through your policy documents for any sign of brutal language like this. Are there clauses that treat anyone in an inhuman manner? Written words are rarely the cause of horrific acts, but they can set the stage and then encourage perpetrators. If you find any unacceptable wording, part of your response will include changing those words into language that fits your organization's culture.

Sometimes organization emergencies present a much more terrifying specter. Good people start to act in disturbing ways, as if they enjoyed harming others. Former friends turn against each other. Your colleagues descend on victims of their abuse as if cruelty was their objective, or turn away when they could have stopped the cruelty. If you have witnessed such behavior, rest assured that it is not unique to your organization. While this is not good news for humans in general, at least it should ease your alarm at what you are facing. Next I will explain some of the reasons good people often brutalize others and, with this understanding, will show how to guide them back to wanting to do good rather than harm.

3.2 How Good People Can Do Very Bad Things

Even good people can do unthinkable things to other people and their organizations. Often, each step that led to a horrific deed seems mundane and hardly worthy of note. The leaders who took them all claim the best intentions—that they were acting in the best interest of the organization. So how can such good, well-intentioned people inflict such unthinkable harm?

Besides my own experiences and encounters with other leaders, I have studied this anomaly in books such as *The Lucifer Effect*, by Philip Zimbardo (2007) and *The Ethical Executive*, by Hoyk and Hersey (2008). Both of these books examine situations where some people committed horrific acts toward others including the Stanford Prison Experiment (1971), Abu Ghraib (2004), and genocide. Dr. Zimbardo was the perpetrator of the Stanford Prison Experiment during which, in just six days, his students devolved into tormentors or cowering subjects depending on the roles he had given them. Somehow he broke the spell and called off the experiment. His personal experience descending into evil and climbing back out makes his book all the more fascinating. The abuse, the ruined careers, and psychological torture that occur within organizations are no less disturbing. Good, ordinary people are easily led into brutality whenever:

The victim has been dehumanized – From the Lucifer Effect website: "Dehumanization is one of the central processes in the transformation of ordinary, normal people into indifferent or even wanton perpetrators of cruelty. Dehumanization is like a 'cortical cataract' that clouds one's thinking and fosters the perception that other people are less than human. It makes some people come to see those others as enemies deserving of torment, torture, and even annihilation."

The offender has been removed from responsibility – Common comments after a malicious act such as firing someone without cause or slandering them to important partners include: I was just following orders, everyone else was doing it, etc. Board members are particularly susceptible to this because most boards of directors are structured to act as a group without individual responsibility.

The system and its people support the brutality – Lack of good policies such as bylaws with clear roles and a fair, respectful executive director agreement; policies that suggest ruthlessness or give special powers to an executive committee; a culture that has set the executive director out as inferior to the board—all of these would support brutality.

Groupthink is enabled – Leaders succumb to the pressure to conform, withholding criticism and avoiding alternatives. Often referred to as "mob mentality," groupthink is usually at the core of tragedies caused by groups. Irving Janis, who studied groupthink extensively, defined it as: "A mode of thinking that people engage in when they are deeply involved in a cohesive in-group, when the members' strivings for unanimity override their motivation to realistically appraise alternative courses of action." Groupthink requires several factors including a charismatic leader, a group of like-minded individuals, a loss of self-awareness, and a culture to always agree. The space shuttle Challenger disaster is one horrific example of groupthink where NASA officials, focused on their cohesive group, ignored warnings from engineers in order to avoid disruption. The near disaster of the Bay of Pigs is also blamed on groupthink within President Kennedy's advisory group. In fact, President Kennedy was so shaken after being caught in groupthink that he set in place policies to prevent it, including requiring differing viewpoints and studying alternatives before finalizing decisions.

Baby steps to blind obedience, usually led by a charismatic authority figure – In the early 1960s a psychology professor at Yale University, Stanley Milgram, set out to learn how German officials and millions of their citizens enabled the Holocaust. He asked for volunteers from the student body and, after repeating the experiment many times, came to a disturbing conclusion. In his article "The Perils of Obedience" (Milgram 1974), he wrote:

> "...Stark authority was pitted against the subjects' strongest moral imperatives against hurting others, and, with the subjects' ears ringing with the screams of the victims, authority won more often than not. The extreme willingness of adults to go to almost any lengths on the command of an authority constitutes the chief finding of the study and the fact most urgently demanding explanation."

Here's how Milgram and others after him set up this obedience experiment, the very same steps leaders of organizations often take before inflicting terrible harm to others:

1. The perpetrators accept a contract with roles and rules such as agreeing to participate in the experiment (could also be an annual executive director contract or a flawed set of bylaws that sets up a brutal system).
2. An authority figure gradually alters the original purpose of the action to allow depravity.
3. This authority figure shows responsibility is diffused away from the perpetrators.
4. A simple first step is followed by steps gradually increasing in harm.
5. There is a gradual change in the nature of the authority figure.
6. There are high exit costs (see groupthink, fear of not conforming).
7. The perpetrators find justification through ideology (authority says it's best for the organization).

Verbal dissent is encouraged – This does nothing to counter the horrific behavior, but works well as an "ego balm" as Dr. Zimbardo likes to call it, further enabling the perpetrator to follow through on the depravity. This could be an apology to the victim for what they "have to do" or a similarly hollow comment as the cruelty is engaged.

Also recognize the harm of inaction. Those who are standing by and thus endorsing the act play a key role. For instance, if a dominant board member calls for the firing of the executive director without cause and the others do not oppose it their inaction has endorsed the offense.

On the other side, those being dehumanized often assist by taking on the role presented by false claims. The Stanford Prison Experiment demonstrated this when previously strong, confident students shrank into cowering outcasts. The system acts on its victims just as it does its perpetrators. It will take all of your compassion and respect to guide them back to being proud of what they have done for your organization.

Heroic action is required to stop these situations. If you are not a leader of the organization, you have to find a hero within the organization to stop this cycle. An outsider or someone who has left the organization's leadership cannot influence leaders who are engulfed in this level of depravity. Also, by guiding the leaders into solving it themselves you will help them gain team confidence for preventing similar situations in the future. If you are one of the leaders, muster all your strength and don your hero's cape.

You as hero will have to seek out at least two supporters before acting. These supporters will keep you from being dismissed as a troublemaker (a form of dehumanization) by the perpetrators. There may be people on your team who have suffered through similar cruelty, but don't expect them to help. They are just as susceptible to inflicting cruelty as the others. I have actually witnessed greater brutality inflicted by those I knew to have been victims of it.

Once you are ready, you will demand evidence of the perpetrators' claims. Defuse their obsession with the present with reminders from the past (examples of the victim's successes) and the future (the mission of the organization). Broadening the scene will often snap complacent group members into becoming heroes. Gather these materials as you prepare your intervention.

Empathize with how these good people were enticed into brutality and show your compassion through your response. Hate the act, not the people carrying it out. Dr. Zimbardo tells of his personal experience inflicting cruelty and the powerful joy he felt when he finally broke the spell to help his victims. Tap the desire for such joy along with the vision of returning the organization to its good work and, I have found, there is a good chance that these good people will turn away from malice.

I once received a call from a board chair, her voice cracking as she explained in broken sentences that she had just fired their organization's executive director. Through gentle questions I learned that she had done this in isolation, in response to actions by the executive that had seemed personally threatening to her. The executive had done nothing that warranted termination. The chair's defense of her action leaned entirely on the structural documents of her organization—an executive director's agreement that allowed the chair to fire, an executive committee structure that gave total power to the chair and two other officers, and bylaws that pitted the board against the executive director. Through her choked-back tears I could hear that she knew these policies were wrong. But it was too late.

I could offer nothing for the disaster that had already occurred. I was there to help her with a different emergency—to guide her into recognizing the danger her organization now faced from this wrongful act and to help her and the remaining leaders of the organization pick up the pieces, including rewriting those unacceptable policies. That organization thrives to this day. I believe their success stemmed from that board chair realizing what a brutal act she had just committed on another human being. Everything she did from then on included preventing that sort of behavior from happening again, even as she had been the perpetrator. Like Dr. Zimbardo, something inside her, an understanding of the difference between right and wrong, had kicked in to reverse the momentum back to good. There was nothing she could do for that unfortunate executive director, but the new policies she and her fellow leaders set in place afterward will save other innocent victims from a similar disgrace.

No matter where you are in the unfolding of your particular crisis, know that taking a stand against abusive behaviors will matter a great deal for the future of your organization. Don't allow it to continue any longer.

First, read on to prepare your stance and response. Even if your organization is only facing minor ailments, learning these response steps will prepare you if you ever do face an organization crisis.

Chapter 4
Before Attempting First Aid

Most people who take leadership positions in organizations do so because they believe they can help their community in that role. Another attraction is working with like-minded people toward a shared goal. Such an enchanting opportunity compares to stepping aboard a three-masted ship to set sail with a hearty crew toward new lands or being chosen to play on a top sports team to fight together for the championship.

When a crisis hits an organization, leaders who still believe in its potential are devastated. Even worse than a medical trauma, they not only feel their own pain, they feel the weight of their entire organization collapsing. Their stress encompasses all the people who helped build the organization and those who rely on it. This might describe you. It may also describe other leaders in the organization who don't realize there is hope.

Because these situations can be so chaotic, with different leaders giving opposing accounts or in hysterics, it is vital that you focus on effective response procedures. They will act as your safe harbor as you venture into the tumult.

4.1 Rules of Response

Before you respond, take note of these two important rules:
#1: Do no harm!

In medical first aid training, this rule is repeated at every turn. In a medical emergency it is easy to see why—anyone rushing in carelessly to try to help can easily cause more damage than if the trauma victim had been left alone until the ambulance arrived. Many people have been paralyzed by well-intentioned helpers moving them carelessly and causing what was initially a curable spinal fracture to sever the spinal cord. Other trauma victims have died because careless helpers have not paid attention to the surroundings and the causes of the trauma such as poison, explosives, or a collapsing building. Well-meaning helpers can heighten the danger through their carelessness or focusing on patient care instead of removing the immediate danger.

Simply by responding, you are adding energy to a volatile situation. If your response is careless in any way, you will do more harm than good.

The next rule pertains to your initial response to the leaders who will often be traumatized.

#2: Make tea and recall the mission.

I learned this tea-making rule during a wilderness response training course because victims of wilderness medical emergencies cannot reach a hospital quickly. This analogy fits organization emergencies because organizations don't have hospitals. All they have is you.

Start by stabilizing the victim and the situation. Then make tea with the group. Guiding people to find firewood, start the fire, fetch the water, find the tea, gather cups, and so on, has a powerful calming effect on the victim and the rest of the group. This alone can save the victim's life, because, after the ABCs (airway, breathing, and circulation), shock is the next most common killer of trauma victims. Calming the situation will lessen shock and will deter other group members from panicking and doing harm.

This is also important with organizations because the organism you are responding to is not just one person, it is the entire organization. If panic (shock) sets in amongst a majority of the leaders, you could face an emergency that cannot be stopped.

The best way to make tea during organization response is

to remind the leaders about their mission. They will likely be on the verge of panic. If they are speaking, they are communicating so they've passed the ABC check and are stable. Slow them down as you would by making tea. Ask them why they originally committed to leading this organization and what their dreams look like when the organization is back on its feet. Encourage them to tell the story in detail by asking pertinent questions just as with all the detailed steps of making tea. Guiding them back to this vision is powerful medicine and could save the organization.

4.2 Responding as One of the Leaders

Even as one of the leaders you will need at least two helpers from the leadership team to join you in your response. This will keep those who are behaving badly from dismissing you as a troublemaker. Depending on how long the crisis has been underway, you should know who is actively causing it, who (besides you) wants it to stop, and who is inactive. The best helpers will obviously be those who are already dismayed by what is happening. But don't forget the silent ones. Even as their inaction is fueling the problem, they still have the potential to help stop it.

Before you contact your potential helpers, gather as much evidence as you can find to support your position. Look especially for records that prove your case against the perpetrators. If they are making wrongful claims against an individual, collect records of that individual's beneficial service to the organization. If they are trying to harm the organization in another way, collect resources both within the organization and from other sources that clearly show that their proposed actions will do significant harm.

With these materials in hand, contact your potential helpers. Remind them of the organization's mission and show them your evidence against the threat. At this point you won't know whether they will assist you, so make your case objectively. Be honest about your level of concern, but leave out emotional judgments. They are just as likely to use your outreach to them to fuel the crisis as they are to help stop it. Stick to the facts.

Once you've summarized your concern, listen carefully to their response and respect any defensive reactions. If they are not yet supportive of your concerns, you will at least find ways to improve your presentation. Check their claims and make any adjustments needed. They may defend the upheaval at first, but if you feel they are open to discussion, contact them again after your further research. Through this one-on-one process you will gain valuable knowledge and hopefully at least two helpers.

You may not find two helpers. Perhaps your leadership team is small or not concerned about the organization. This will make your response much more difficult. Read the next chapter expecting to respond by yourself, but never stop seeking helpers. If you've seen the movie *12 Angry Men* keep that story in mind. One brave juror stood his ground for due process even as the other eleven jurors demanded the death penalty and a quick end to the effort. Finally, in the end, they understood that he was right and the innocent man was released. As your own story unfolds, some who first defend bad behavior can change their minds. That movie is a classic portrayal of groupthink and it shows graphically how a single hero can break its spell. The hero can take the place of the malicious authority figure and lead the others back to empathy for their victim.

Outside supporters and staff members, other than the executive director, cannot help directly because they have no authority over the organization. You may know outsiders who have powerful influence over some of your fellow leaders, but encouraging their involvement would be inappropriate. In fact, if an outsider has been making decisions for any leader, they could be at the root of the problem and any encouragement could make it worse. Remember, do no harm. Resist the temptation to contact these influential outsiders. If they are funders, officials, or partners you will not only tempt them into inappropriate action, you may undermine or ruin their previously beneficial relationship with the organization.

4.3 Responding as a Non-Leader, Victim, or Employee

If you are not a leader of the organization, your role will be to guide its leaders into solving the emergency themselves. You cannot take a lead role in the response. This way, not only will you help them through the immediate danger, you will show them they can solve a crisis together.

As a funder, your job will be all the more difficult because the leaders will tend to hold back unflattering details in order to remain eligible for your funding. As an employee, you will be accused of overstepping your duties. As the victim, you will be dismissed as defensive or hysterical; your attempts to defend yourself will be used as proof of their claims.

In any of these cases or as an outsider, you will need to catch the attention of at least one leader and persuade them to become the hero. Gather all the supportive information you can to make your case. Always try to connect with more than one leader. Since most emergencies are related to power struggles, reaching just one leader could be perceived as favoritism.

You can calm a leader simply by asking what the world will be like after their organization has completed its mission. This works much like the rule of making tea. It places the emergency into perspective by reminding those involved of the long-term effects of their work.

You may learn very personal details about the leaders you work with. You will also be bombarded with gossip and half-truths. Never repeat or forward any of this information, even if someone asks. Also, never tell others that the organization is facing an emergency as this would add to their crisis. Don't mention it even after it is resolved. Your success depends on gaining the trust of the leaders and that usually means that others never find out about it.

Even if you think you have a good idea for a solution that is not cloned from indiscriminate nonprofit sources, always hesitate before offering your advice. The best solutions always come from the leaders themselves, so respond instead with questions that will guide the leaders toward solving the problem themselves.

As you work through these discussions, be patient. Leaders fighting for survival are often distracted. Slow the conversation down. No matter how bizarre, or even minor, their concern seems, listen and respond with respect. Leaders often leave out clarifying details in the heat of a crisis. Other times their concern will be based solely on their intuition. As you read in Chapter 2, many of the symptoms that lead to emergencies seem minor taken by themselves. So always trust the intuition of leaders and treat them, and their concerns, with the utmost respect.

As an outsider working through the leaders, you might miss important interactions. This is okay as long as there's progress toward a solution. You might even miss the conclusion. Signs that the leaders have found their feet include correcting you with what they believe is an even better solution than the one you had discussed with them. My heart always leaps with joy when I check in with an organization and the leader nonchalantly describes the much better solution they already implemented, then notes how terribly busy they are. I congratulate them, all the while holding back my cheers until I've hung up.

Now we can move into first aid for crises and after that, remedies for ailments. In the next chapter, I will offer common first aid treatments. Every step of the way, write thorough notes. Keep these well into the future to avoid similar situations and to assist with emergencies elsewhere. By committing to help struggling organizations you will be part of a new expectation that good organizations should be saved. Eventually this may lead to the creation of a response system as effective as our medical response system is today.

Section 2

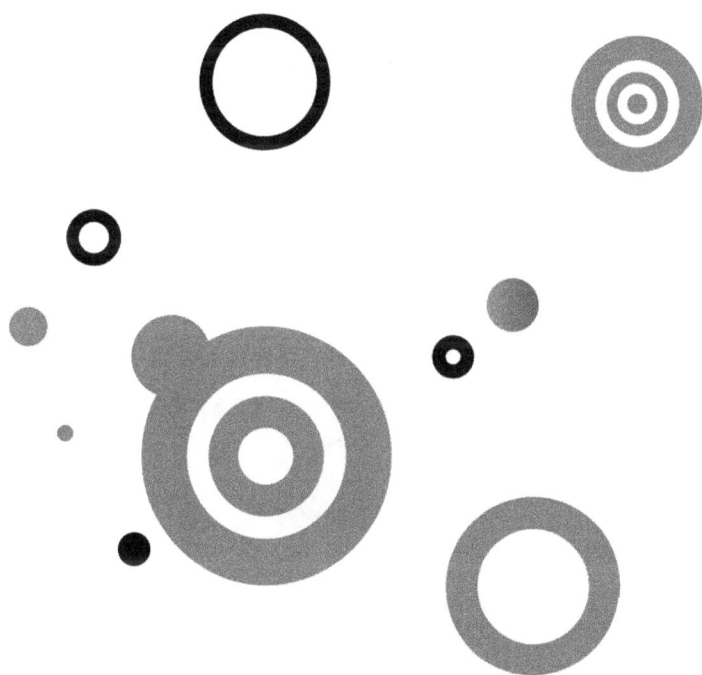

First Aid and Remedies

Chapter 5
First Aid for Organizations in Crisis

Anyone who has taken a first aid course or witnessed a medical team responding to an emergency will know the level of professionalism and accuracy required to save lives. Trained professionals follow a strict regimen that keeps them focused even in the midst of terrifying scenarios. Their training drills include distractions like gushing fake blood, raging fires, and screaming family members. They are trained to shut out these emotional triggers and focus entirely on their particular role. The commander stays on the periphery so he or she can see the entire scene and assign jobs to the rest of the team members.

You and your response team will need similar focus when responding to an emergency. We will look at remedies for less-threatening ailments later because emergencies need to be resolved first. You will not have the luxury of accredited training drills, but do take the time to sit down together to discuss what you know about the situation and run through potential scenarios. This will build confidence that you can indeed respond professionally and effectively.

Keep your organization's mission front and center throughout the entire response. An ailment, even at the crisis level, is defined by the inability to focus energy on the organization's purpose. Restored health will mean that energy can once again flow toward that important work. That vision will help each of you shut out inevitable, disturbing distractions.

While there is an abundance of resources available for nourishing healthy organizations—books, workshops, consultants, and many free materials—don't expect these healthful resources to assist during an emergency. You wouldn't hand an apple to someone who just fell off a cliff. Neither should you hand a book on board development to a leader trying to cope with warring board factions.

I have one more thought to offer before we get into response steps. Most of the time organizations in crisis should be revived. However, for some this might not be the best solution. Perhaps an organization was founded for an inappropriate or unimportant reason that no one cares about. It may have been innocently founded as a redundant organization and a merger is not possible. Or it may have been founded with great intentions that end up doing harm. In any of these cases, a graceful disbanding of the organization is the best option.

The situation could be worse. You might discover it was founded to harm others. This can occur when a faction from one organization founds an identical organization in retaliation. Any work toward that redundant mission does harm not only toward the original organization, but to the entire cause they supposedly share. Others are more obvious such as racist groups or those that perpetuate the abuse of other beings. You will have to draw your own line of tolerance. If the organization you are considering helping reveals behaviors that cross your line, you have two possible responses that are very different from first aid: 1) walk away or, 2) actively work to disband the organization.

If you choose the second option, you will become their assailant. Do your best to empathize with their perspective. As you read on through the first aid steps, imagine their desperation as they respond to your effort to shut them down. Do not engage in such an attack unless you are absolutely certain the organization you are targeting is doing significant harm. If you're not sure or if you believe they could shift their work to become beneficial, start by offering to help them do so.

Now let's get into first aid response steps.

5.1 Responding to Any Emergency
5.1.1 Any Emergency, Step One: Identify Threats

Scan the entire scene, not just your immediate surroundings, but the whole community where your organization does work. What caused the emergency? Who is actively doing harm? Who is helping respond to the threat? Who is complacent? Who can help?

Take note of anyone actively trying to do your organization harm. Many times they will believe they are acting in the best interest of the community. Perhaps they think that stealing one of your programs to lead it themselves will be the best thing for that program. Sometimes attackers, acting on misinformation, will gather an angry mob. Such assailants can be part of your team or outside of your organization.

Others could include leaders of a long-dead organization blocking your work. I refer to these as "zombie attacks." Also look at the history of your community to find out if a similar organization failed in the past, leaving a residue of doubt and distrust for any organization that attempts that sort of work. I refer to these as "toxic waste sites."

More obvious attackers are your true opponents as well as thieves either within or outside of your organization. They will justify their actions, but don't be tempted to respond to false claims. Focus on stopping their harm.

Nonhuman threats can include brutal policy language, a flawed mission statement, and too few or too many policies. You and your fellow leaders cannot change these until the crisis is over, but at least you can note that they are contributing.

Scan the whole picture, check your notes from your diagnosis process in Chapter 2, and note every threat you find.

5.1.2 Any Emergency, Step Two: Secure the Scene
        Once you have identified all threats, you need to secure
the scene so that you and your helpers can administer first aid in
safety without causing further harm. Do what you can to block
further attacks. Notify authorities of any illegal activities including
threatening behaviors as well as theft of money or property.
Depending on the emergency and who is involved, inform your
fellow leaders of the problem and its current status.

5.2 Responding to Factions and Rogues
5.2.1 Factions and Rogues, Step One: Investigate and Gather
Materials
        Fully investigate all the people involved. Find out who is
causing the harm. Do they have assistants? Who is trying to stop
the attack? Who is complacent? Who can help stop the attack?
        Find out all pertinent details about the people you identify,
including organizations and businesses they are affiliated with
that might explain their motivation. Look through all of your
organization's policy documents to identify any that may have
encouraged their behavior.
        Legal action is rarely successful in these situations, but
record every step along the way just in case you must resort to it.

5.2.2 Factions and Rogues, Step Two: Find Two Helpers
        Find at least two helpers from the leadership team. If you
must respond alone, you will have to adapt these processes and
lower your expectations for success. If you are an outsider, staff
member, or the victim, you will need a hero on the leadership
team who is ready to lead the response. Make sure your helpers
understand the urgency and are fully committed to responding.
The best helpers will be those who are already dismayed by what
is happening. Don't forget the silent ones. Even as their inaction is
fueling the problem, they may eventually decide to help.
        Brief your helpers in a private meeting to examine all the
supportive material each of you have found. Then combine your

collective knowledge into an overview of the situation and prepare to present it to the other leaders.

5.2.3 Factions and Rogues, Step Three: Discuss Concerns with ALL Leaders

If the assailants are leaders of the organization, this will be extremely awkward for you and your helpers. It's still paramount that you bring together the entire leadership team to present your concerns and discuss the crisis in a professional and objective manner. At best, this can resolve the problem. At worst, you can record it as due diligence. In case the emergency has gone on so long that factions have drawn territorial lines, choose a neutral location, such as a library meeting room rather than the office, for your in-person meeting.

There is a chance that such a meeting, if conducted with respect and empathy for all the leaders, could resolve the problem, so go in with this high expectation. Set meeting rules at the start, assign a note taker, and ensure that everyone has a chance to speak. Do not accuse anyone of wrongdoing even in your invitation to the meeting. Even if you know that one of the leaders has committed a terrible act, as long as that act was not illegal (in which case the appropriate authorities should be taking charge), present the results of that act objectively. I like to use passive voice in these situations. For example: "Our top funder was told that our organization cannot handle their grant" instead of "Bob told our top funder..." Allow the discussion to reveal how this occurred. Then give this person a chance to explain their actions and correct them.

Stick to your agenda and target time for this meeting. If the problem cannot be solved at that meeting, schedule another within the next few days. Continue these meetings until a resolution can be formulated that is acceptable to the entire leadership team. This will avoid bolstering factions caused by a vote under majority rule and its divisive win/lose structure.

In the unfortunate circumstance that some leaders refuse

to attend such meetings, hold the meetings anyway and keep the internal communication channels open to all leaders, even those who boycott the meetings. These should include frequent, objective updates that are void of blaming and finger pointing.

5.2.4 Factions and Rogues, Step Four: Resolve and Repair

These meetings will unearth disturbing details, all of which you will have to work together to resolve. Some people may have to be asked to step down from their leadership roles. Others may have to be set to work on cleaning up a mess they created. You and all other leaders should support these people in what they have to do. Offer help and guidance. Even if they must step down, make this process as respectful, empathetic, and educational as possible. Thank them for any positive contributions they have made to the organization.

There is a chance that even after many meetings, factions will remain in conflict. Gauge your personal tolerance for continuing the effort to restore the organization. When you are nearing the end of your endurance, sit down once again with your helpers to discuss options. You might have to walk away. Take care of yourself as you are important to the cause you are trying to serve. If you step away from a hopeless situation before you are personally traumatized, you can offer your energy and skills through another, more effective channel.

More likely, after a few of these meetings, all of you will return to your previous team spirit, relieved that the drama is over. Immediately stop any harmful external communication that may have occurred during the crisis. If such communication did go out, send out an honest yet relieved update to the recipients. Keep this update objective and free of any names of wrongdoers. Then schedule regular external communications that report on the good work you will now be able to return to. Find a fun way to show appreciation for all the leaders who pulled the organization through the crisis, then work to nurture their team spirit.

5.2.5 Factions and Rogues, Step Five: Create Policies to Prevent Recurrence

Don't get too comfortable before all of you have corrected or created policies that will prevent such crises from recurring. Gather any suspect policies you discovered during your investigations. Also note any missing policies that could have contained the problem before it spun out of control. Keep your policy documents to the minimum to avoid redundancy and confusion. These should include:

- Bylaws that clarify roles and responsibilities as well as removal procedures for any leader found to be doing harm (including through inaction) that applies to all leaders, including the executive director, and requires the full support of all leaders;
- An executive director's agreement that points to the removal section in your bylaws as the only policy for their removal;
- Employee agreements and an employee manual that clearly state rules and responsibilities that protect the organization from misbehavior; and
- Roles clearly distinguished in bylaws and employee job descriptions to keep people out of roles not appropriate for them.

As soon as everyone has recovered, call another special meeting with your fellow leaders and get to work revising and writing the policies you need to protect your organization from danger. More details about these policies are covered later.

5.3 Responding to Outside Threats

5.3.1 Outside Threats, Step One: Stop Threats Controlled by Your Organization

Sometimes outside threats are fueled by intentional or unintentional actions from your organization. Perhaps an external communication or web post used offensive or inappropriate language that set off an attack. Other times a rogue leader or staff member may have started their own crusade against the organization. Immediately put a stop to any of these activities. Remove harmful language or send out corrections. Fire staff members who are leading such an attack. Do this swiftly yet with empathy for their situation. Confront rogue leaders for their inappropriate behavior, then assemble a special meeting of all leaders to deal with this person.

5.3.2 Outside Threats, Step Two: Respond Directly to Those Doing Harm

Once threats under your control have been dealt with, respond to any outsiders leading an attack. Keep your response confidential, ideally in person with the assailants, along with a written complaint regarding their activities. This will act as your record of notice and will be important if legal action becomes necessary. Meet them in a safe setting and bring along witnesses in case of violence. Depending on your level of concern, especially if they have threatened anyone, you might want to request that an officer from the appropriate authority accompany you and your helpers to the encounter.

No matter what unfolds, follow due process. Start by allowing the person a means of remedying their harm. Ask them if they meant to cause this harm. By asking questions you will show them appropriate respect and the benefit of the doubt. There is a chance they acted out of ignorance or to impress someone else; that they had no idea of the level of damage they caused. Allow them the opportunity to do the right thing by apologizing and assisting in a remedy.

Record the outcome of this first meeting and any other results. Recognize that they have a tendency toward bad behavior and they could do it again.

Making your response confidential will at least keep your part in it respectful and out of the public eye. However, people who attack organizations out of ignorance and personal enjoyment will tend to take the discussion public. Be prepared for this when you write out your concern for them. Write it as if it will be publicized and adjust every word with your team to ensure there is no trace of anything that will harm your organization. Keep it objective and open to the possibility that this person did not mean to do harm.

After your initial response, if they continue their hostilities, you may need to involve an attorney. There may be one in your circle of supporters who would like to help. A follow-up response from an attorney noting the due diligence you and your team have followed can do wonders for quieting hostile people.

5.3.3 Outside Threats, Step Three: Increase Good Work and Promote Emphatically

After responding to your assailants, even in a "toxic waste site," focus on increasing your good work and describing it through frequent, positive external communications sent more often than usual. Continue these extra communications for at least two months so that most people in your community will have a true context for any false claims your assailants may have made. These newsworthy snippets should go out in many forms including e-newsletters, press releases, posts to other websites, personal appearances, and events around your community. You won't know for sure when your organization's reputation has been restored, so err on the side of caution and keep this confident, yet honest communication flowing at double-time as long as you can.

5.4 Responding to Funding Crises
5.4.1 Funding, Step One: Speak with Funder

Funding crises come in several forms. Most common is a shortage, but inappropriate funding can be just as harmful. A much more critical situation is when significant funding has been stolen or misused. First, as with the responses outlined above, fully investigate everything that led to the problem. In the case of inappropriate funding, find out why it was pursued, who approved it, and all the circumstances involved in the deal. If you uncover theft or misuse, find out who is responsible and call the appropriate authorities immediately. Once the case is in their hands, you will want to inform your funder.

In the other cases, with all the pertinent information in hand and your fellow leaders updated, speak with the funder. If they refused to give funding that you had expected, ask them why. Distinguish this situation from your expected number of denied grants—you can only hope for one out of ten perfect proposals to be accepted. In contrast, this sort of crisis comes about when a funder had promised funding and then withheld it. By asking them why they withheld their funding you may learn about ailments within your organization that need treatment. You may also find out that the funder encountered their own problems that had nothing to do with your side of the relationship.

Supposing that you cannot pay back a loan by its deadline, your first response step is the same—speak with the lender. Be direct. Tell them the truth. There's a chance they will extend the deadline. If not, you will have to face whatever consequences were spelled out in the loan agreement. By contacting the lender promptly and well before the deadline, at least you will show them that your organization is professional and respects their.

In a case where inappropriate funding was accepted by one of your leaders or staff members, your response to the funder will be a very delicate affair. This is made all the worse if leaders actively sought the inappropriate funding, referred to as "chasing the money." Leaders who chase the money are harming their organization and need to be dealt with as rogues, noted earlier in this chapter. Another serious situation may arise through your investigation of a funding crisis—that the organization was founded for the sole purpose of obtaining charity funding, no matter what that funding is for. Chances are you will know whether your organization is an illegal sham like these, but take the care to fully investigate.

An example of a well-meaning but inappropriate funding situation could be an organization with a mission to plant and care for street trees in a certain city. A funder offers $50,000 to this small organization whose annual budget is lucky to reach that amount. The problem is the funder requires that the funding be used to build a bike path through a park. This has nothing to do with street trees or their care. If a leader or staff member of this street tree organization were to accept this funding it would put the organization into immediate peril because most of its infrastructure—staff, volunteers, office, supplies, promotional materials—would have to shift over to building the bike path. Their street tree efforts would be abandoned.

When facing a similar emergency, call a meeting with your kind funder. Start by apologizing for the mix-up. Then fully present the mission and vision of your organization. Bring your organization to life for them. From there you can show them why their specific project does not fit your organization's work. Then be quiet to allow them time to process this information. Most likely they will accept your check returning their funding. There is a potential that they will decide to fund your organization anyway, removing the inappropriate stipulations and allowing their funding to go toward one of your projects that is already in your work plan.

Other funding troubles can be caused by failed fundraising drives and events. In these cases, your organization is entirely responsible for the emergency, so there is no one else to approach. You'll read about succeeding with fundraising drives and events later in the book. Most importantly, avoid launching one unless you are certain of success and always keep your fundraising goals low for events. Better to be pleasantly surprised, than come up short.

5.4.2 Funding, Step Two: Tap Inner Circle of Supporters

When funding cannot be recovered, your next step will be to examine every planned expense in your work plan/budget for that year. Work with your fellow leaders to find every penny that can be cut to make up for the shortage. Meet with your staff members to explain the situation and ask them what they can do without. To avoid laying off people, ask if they can work one or two days fewer each week. Postpone upgrades and ask employees to manage with existing equipment until the crisis has passed.

Next, reach out to your inner circle of supporters—starting with board members. Ask your fellow leaders to give as much as they possibly can and then give just a bit more. Present this request as you write out your own check in an amount that causes you the level of pain you are requesting from them. After this, if all of you have not covered the shortage, seek contributions from your most supportive and trusted donors with one-on-one private discussions. These people must be the sort who can hear bad news and not flee from your organization. Make this distinction carefully because you do not want the news of your funding crisis to repel any of your current supporters or worse, be leaked to the media and spread around your community.

5.4.3 Funding, Step Three: Create Policies and Procedures to Prevent Recurrence

After filling the funding gap, you and your fellow leaders need to sit down and hammer out policies and procedures that will prevent similar disasters in the future. Keep your financial policy documents to the minimum to avoid redundancy and confusion. These should include:

- A concise work plan/budget created and passed each year,
- Employee agreements that specify fundraising responsibilities,
- An employee manual that includes proper procedures for working with funders,
- A bookkeeping system that accurately tracks all income and expenses.

Another place you should look is your communication systems. If your funding emergency was a result of funders not understanding the work of your organization, allocate the time to improve all of your promotions so funders will be less likely to offer inappropriate funding or pull out of their promises.

Having to administer first aid, no matter what the circumstance, is not pleasant. But the outcome can be quite rewarding when you understand the level of danger you have averted.

An executive director called me once to let me know he was moving to a distant city. With upbeat words he described the opportunities that lay ahead for him. But between those colorful descriptions I recognized a dark undertone. He had not mentioned his board members and he'd said nothing about the organization he was leaving behind. Carefully, I wove these questions in, and yet, even with my care, he broke down.

His voice now quivering, he told me of the months-long descent to animosity that he and his board had endured. It had begun with a simple communication breakdown when the board had given too much power to a consultant. This executive had slowly slipped away from his board until he had reached the breaking point. His move to the new city was only the finale of a diabolical plan he was ready to deploy. He was going to leave his organization in ruins for the shame his board had bestowed on him. This was not an entertaining call about his travels. He had called from the ledge right before a leap that would have crushed him and a good organization.

Even as my heart raced, I found an outward calm. Because I had begun my respectful inquiries early in our conversation, I was able to continue the thread without startling him. I broadened the scope of my questions to help him remember all the accomplishments he and his organization had achieved toward their mission over the years. Then I asked him to describe some of the new projects he and his board had planned together. When I finally heard his breathing slow and tenderness replace deceit, I asked him to describe the best way he could leave his organization to ensure that his board and a new executive would meet those goals and flourish together. He went on to implement that positive plan and a month after our call, his board of directors threw him a tear-filled going-away party. They never found out about his original plan.

No matter how disturbing the crisis may be, respond. Do so immediately in the most professional, objective, and kind manner you and your helpers can muster. Also seek personal support from your friends and family to ease your own stress through the ordeal. The thought of responding may make your guts churn, but in the end the result can feed your soul and rescue your organization for many more generations of good work.

Now that you have learned effective first aid procedures, let's look at simple remedies for more common ailments. Treating these familiar annoyances is nowhere near as dramatic as responding to a life-threatening situation. In fact, treating ailments can seem downright boring in comparison. Don't let that fool you. Each and every one of the ailments you'll read about next contains the potential of a full-blown crisis if left untreated. Take them seriously and mop them up as soon as you can.

Chapter 6
People, Purpose, and Public Image Remedies

As we examine particular remedies, place them in the context of your organization as a whole. Just as a skin rash can be treated with an ointment, it can also signify systemic ailments that require comprehensive treatment if not an entire lifestyle change. Especially note the remedies that align with the ailments you checked in the diagnostic chapter.

You and your fellow leaders may have found creative ways to adapt to ailments that have been there so long, you no longer consider them problems. Perhaps you've managed without an executive director as each of you has covered daily tasks and even staff oversight on your "off" time. Perhaps you've operated for years without bylaws because all of you know your mission statement, policies, and procedures by heart and you believe there's no reason to put them down in writing since no new leaders have joined you. I know from personal experience that many disabled people can adapt to their disabilities to such an extent that their disabilities are hardly noticed. The difference is that you have the choice to remove your organization's ailments. Unless you can find a truly beneficial reason for keeping an ailment, I highly recommend ridding your organization of it. Don't be tempted to defend anything that can hold your organization back from reaching its potential.

6.1 People Remedies

Ailments caused by people are either emergencies or can easily escalate to that level. The most obvious are when a lone leader or employee is taking independent action and when separate factions are working against each other. Follow the first aid procedures covered in the previous chapters before working through these more straightforward remedies.

I'll start with problems involving factions and rogues that have not yet reached a crisis level. We'll also look at confusion over roles and common ailments involving boards of directors and executive directors.

6.1.1 Factions and Rogues

Factions and rogues are the most common people ailments and the most likely to escalate into a crisis. Even with policies in place, you are still facing a very unpleasant situation. The first step is to find out who is causing the harm.

Discuss your concerns, either alone with the lone perpetrator or, if this is a faction, with all leaders. Request an open discussion and ask for solutions so that all of you can return to your good work. Refer to the mission statement to remind this person or group why all of you are there. This should help keep the discussion away from name calling and petty details.

You may discover that one board member acted independently for their own benefit. Distinguish between healthy, contrary viewpoints that should be encouraged and rogue behavior that seeks personal gain. Some examples include misleading partners into contracts that benefit the board member's own company or using the organization's name to lure clients to their separate business dealings. Others can do more direct harm, such as presenting unapproved initiatives to government officials.

For an employee, if the offense was not extreme, they need an immediate, clear warning in writing from the executive director. Even for a board member, I recommend putting your warning in writing so you can refer to it later. Then ensure the solutions are implemented. If not, you will have to turn to your policies such as your bylaws or employee manual.

In the case of a misbehaving employee, they may need to be fired. Go through the warning process first because even the best employees can do stupid things. Note patterns because minor offenses repeated over time, like arriving late every day or ignoring duties, can add up to major harm. Once or twice is understandable and a warning should remedy it, but repeated many times, even after a warning, points to an entrenched behavioral problem.

If their offense was extreme, don't bother with a warning. Drinking on the job, badmouthing the organization, and stealing are some of the behaviors that have tipped the scale for me. Refer to their job description and your employee manual to show them how their misconduct has caused harm. Do your best to make them appreciate being fired. Your organization was not founded to devastate people, not even those with the worst behavior problems. Being hired may have been one of their proudest moments. To be fired could throw them into unimaginable depths. Make it part of your organization's culture that if someone must be let go, the process will be as respectful, compassionate, and educational as it can possibly be.

As a leader of organizations and as a bike shop owner I have had to go through this gut wrench far too many times. I start by letting them know the situation is serious, taking them to a private room and asking them what they expected would happen when they did what they did. If I had given them a warning and they repeated their offense, I point to that warning in writing. I let them do most of the talking and by the time we both stand up, they have basically fired themselves quite happily. Employees who do harm to your organization often do so because they are no longer interested in the job, but don't have the courage to quit. Being fired, if it is done respectfully, can come as a great relief to them.

When faced with factions or a rogue board member and your first meeting did not work, it's time to stop their disruption. Gather all the leaders who are not engaged in subversion to discuss remedies based on your policies. When you confront the offenders, adhere to kindness and respect even as you inform them that they must step down from their leadership role. The people engaged in destructive behavior likely joined the leadership team to assist. Something has changed, but those original intentions should not be forgotten.

Remedies for recharging the energy of your organization after removing rogues and factions will center on communication and the resulting public image you and your team create.

6.1.2 Role Confusion

At best, role confusion wastes energy. At worst, it infuriates those who understand their own role and can lead to factions. The most prevalent confusion is between the roles of board members and the executive director. Board members focus on broad governance as a group while the executive director oversees daily tasks that ensure the organization reaches their chosen goals. When these roles are confused, board members micromanage the executive director and give orders to other employees who should only be answering to the executive director.

No board of directors can effectively manage employees in positions lower than the executive director. This is because a board of directors needs to operate as a group—in other words, no individuals acting without the consent of the entire board. For efficiency and to avoid confusion, employees must receive their directions from only one person. Placing a board member into a supervisory role will either force them to make inappropriate decisions necessary for directing staff or, if they attempt to avoid this, will bring the organization to a standstill.

This is why the first employee you hire should be your executive director. Also, do not make the mistake of hiring someone to a lower position and expecting them to perform executive director duties. Their lower pay and, more importantly, their lesser title will cause them to resent the board and may entice them to retaliate. Once your executive director is in place, all board members will have to respect the executive's role of day-to-day decision making.

An important remedy for executive director/board member role confusion is a bylaws update. Proper bylaws clearly differentiate these roles even as they place these leaders at an equal level of responsibility. You'll read more about bylaws upgrades in the next chapter.

Roles are also confused when staff and volunteers are placed in the wrong role for their skills and personalities. Someone who applies for a job may not understand its day-to-day duties. Their resume might match, but once they start, it becomes clear they are not a good fit. When a volunteer's expertise is overlooked they can easily be placed into a role they do not want.

Experts are rarely interested in being leaders, so don't force them onto your board or consider them for the executive director position. Imagine a shy technical person placed in the role of public spokesperson or a high energy person who wants hands-on work with clients only discussing that work in meetings. This not only happens with volunteers and employees. Countless board members accept the role believing they will be actively involved in programs, not attending governance meetings and studying budgets. Some people can be both an expert and a leader, but first be sure of their leadership ability before asking them to serve in that role.

Once you discover someone in the wrong role, respond promptly. Discuss the issue with them and find a way to shift them into a more suitable role. If an employee shows great potential, consider creating a new position just so you can keep them. Excellent employees are hard to find so this investment could be well worth it. For board members, shift them off of the board and into a volunteer program position that interests them.

6.1.3 Boards of Directors and Committees

In order to function properly, a board needs to work as a group to oversee the broad, long-term goals that serve the organization's mission.

Ailments involving board members generally result from either missing or flawed policies. A common flaw is the concept of "executive committees." Executive committees are usually formed with a small number of board members in order to complete a specific task. This is not a problem as long as such a committee is not allowed to make decisions for the entire organization. Unfortunately, because of their title, executive committees tend to mutate into all-powerful bodies; in other words, officially sanctioned factions. This often starts as a band-aid solution to boards that grow past the ideal maximum of twelve.

In the case that your board has ballooned past twelve, do not be tempted to slice out an executive committee in order to get work done. At least do not call it an executive committee because this term is dangerously misleading. Creating any sub-group of the board that is given full decision-making power endorses a faction. Also, never create an executive committee in lieu of hiring an executive director. Until your executive director is hired, the entire board will remain responsible for all decisions—overarching as well as day-to-day.

Committees of the board can take on preliminary work for projects, but should be expected to bring their drafts back to the entire board for final decisions. Minor decisions are fine such as small purchases, but not decisions that significantly impact the organization. Name such committees for their tasks—the Employee Manual Committee or the Fundraising Event Committee or the Grant Research Committee—but avoid any term like "executive" that suggests full power over the organization. Add language to your bylaws that prevents any committee from making decisions for the entire organization.

6.1.4 Inviting New Board Members

Many ailments result when people who have no experience with an organization are elected to its board. This often follows recommendations to seek board members with particular skills (legal, management, political, etc.). People who are not committed to the success of an organization can easily justify doing it harm.

The only way to know if someone is committed to the success of your organization is after they have taken part in its activities, without any expectation of a leadership role. Set up a system that ensures many people can take active roles in your organization, through volunteer programs, special events and committees. Very few people are leaders or even want to be in a leadership role. As you work with your volunteers and helpers, keep an eye out for those offering big ideas for the benefit of the entire organization. If their ideas take into account the organization's current form and build on it, they could be leadership quality. Other skills such as legal, management, and event planning are secondary.

A similar mistake occurs when leaders need the assistance of an expert such as an attorney or accountant. Instead of approaching them with a distinct request such as filing official papers or doing taxes, these leaders invite the expert to serve on their board of directors. This is akin to needing someone to help you build a shed and instead asking them to tutor your children— apples and oranges. Experts need to focus on their specialties. Board service is a huge responsibility entailing regular meetings and constant examination of the entire organization. Don't divert your experts into this arduous task. In fact, most will understand the difference and will decline to serve, thus shutting the door to their expert services.

Make board development an ongoing effort to keep your number of board members in that effective zone between five and twelve. When you need to bring in new board members, don't fixate on "board recruitment," which suggests invitations to inappropriate people. Focus instead on communicating achievements and creating fun activities that attract many diverse people to take part in your organization's work simply as participants and volunteers. Then keep an eye out for those special people who show these three critical characteristics:

1. They fully understand and adore your organization's purpose—this can be demonstrated through pertinent questions and offering to further the mission;
2. They are taking part in its activities—e.g., showing up to events and meetings, offering to volunteer, inviting their friends to get involved; and
3. They exhibit leadership skills—e.g., showing interest in the organization as a whole, offering ideas to help it reach its vision well into the future, identifying potential barriers to the mission, and similar governance-related abilities.

Discourage board invitations to anyone unless they meet all three of these criteria. You may already know people who do. Otherwise, creating welcoming activities that attract many varied people will also attract the people you need on your board. Include a requirement for prior involvement with the organization in your bylaws.

6.1.5 Executive Director

Setting the position of executive director as time-limited or as a contract position are common mistakes, signaling a lack of confidence in hiring this top staff position.

An organization needs an executive director when it reaches a certain level of growth and significance. Many small organizations that have low-impact purposes will always function well with only a volunteer board of directors at their helm. These are often social clubs or local associations whose mission statements spell out very little impact on society. Their inward energy only needs to match their low outward energy in order to keep a healthy, beneficial balance.

However, if your organization has a mission statement that expects high impact for the community it serves and you have reached a point where the volunteer board cannot do a good job

with necessary day-to-day tasks, it's time to hire an executive
director. Avoid hiring program staff or administrative staff until
you have an executive director on your payroll. A volunteer board
cannot manage employees and employees, other than the executive
director, should never be given leadership duties that encompass
the entire organization. Only an executive director can fill this role.
Pay them a market-rate salary that falls in the range of executive
director salaries of similar organizations in your area so they will
stay with you a long time.

You might tremble even at the thought of paying someone
any amount of money, let alone a market rate salary for an
executive director. To ease your qualms, realize that the executive
director's main job is to ensure that the organization reaches the
goals set out in the annual work plan and budget that was passed
by the entire board at the start of the year. If that budget includes
a market-rate salary for the executive director then it is their job
to ensure that funding is secured. Making your executive director
a voting member of the board also smoothes this concern because
they will be part of the work plan and budget discussion including
identifying reasonable and likely sources of funding that will cover
their salary. Make them part of that discussion and decision process
so that they will not only understand the reasoning behind the
fundraising plan, they will take ownership in its success.

Another ailment occurs when the wrong person is hired as
executive director. This will become clear within the first three to
six months after they are hired. Do not confuse this ailment with
a much more serious crisis covered earlier—when an executive
director who is doing a good job is torpedoed by self-serving
board members. This mismatch will be clear to everyone, even
people outside of the organization. A bad hire can occur when
the applicant misunderstands the job requirements and the board
members doing the hiring don't look past a stunning resume. While
a mismatch in a lower staff position is disturbing, a mismatch for
executive director is worse because you have placed this person in
a leadership role and given them the keys to the entire organization

so they can carry out its day-to-day operations. Your executive director must have access to the organization's bank account so they can ensure bills are paid and deposits made. They also must be given full power to hire, manage, and even fire employees.

As a board member with various organizations over the years, I have been involved in the hiring of three bad choices for executive director. Fortunately, all three were good people at heart, simply bad matches for a leadership role. Two resolved this problem themselves. In the first months on the job, they stopped doing anything, like deer in the headlights. They knew as well as anyone they were not fit for the job and, even as we board members began discussing the problem, they resigned. The other was much more difficult to deal with. She stayed on the job for several years trying her best to do the work she had no experience or interest in. This caused her great stress, which transferred to the other staff members and seeped into the public image of the organization. Because she was trying, we let her continue. Finally, she too resigned. Looking back, I realize we as the board should have acted on this earlier, perhaps finding her a lesser staff position in which she could use her program skills and not be troubled by leadership duties.

The best way to avoid such situations is to hire someone who has already been actively involved in your organization. This could be a volunteer, a board member, or a current employee who has proven their leadership abilities along with their passion for the organization's success. Alternatively, you could include a break-in period, perhaps six months, along with a different title like interim director with its own agreement that outlines goals they must reach. If the goals aren't met, even they will understand why they have to leave.

Remedies for poor executive director choices should include a clear job description included in their executive director agreement. Their job description will keep them on track and will be the means of demonstrating whether or not they are doing their job.

In the unfortunate case that your executive director is on contract or has a time-limited agreement, change this immediately to a regular employee agreement that expects them to be around for a long time. You'll find more details in the next chapter.

If you are not paying your executive director at market rate for your area, discuss how they can work with the board to raise the funds needed to increase their salary. Great executive directors are eager for challenges and this one brings with it a direct benefit to them.

6.1.6 Contractors

Contractors fill an entirely different role and should not be considered staff or employees. They are self-employed specialists such as your accountant, your plumber, and your website designer. Your organization can hire them to do a finite job as long as that job is not a primary aspect of the work you do. Unlike an employee, you cannot control how they perform that job. This is part of the legal description of a contractor in the United States and some other countries. Your contract with them is for the completion of a project, not how they complete it. You also cannot hire a contractor for open-end work, this being part of the legal description of an employee. It must be a defined job that will be completed in a certain amount of time. While their expert advice can be added to leader discussions, contractors should never be allowed to influence your organization. This all means that your executive director cannot be a contractor

Sometimes employee agreements are wrongfully referred to as employee contracts. This causes serious confusion. Use the term "contract" only for contractors.

Working with contractors can be enticing because they are responsible for handling all their own bookkeeping. All you have to do is pay them. Because of this, many leaders of young nonprofits make the mistake of hiring their executive director and other regular staff as contractors. In the United States, this is *illegal*! (See irs.gov Publication 15-A.) It will set your organization up for fines and back payment of employee taxes. A contractor is a sole proprietor, in business for themselves. They are expected to be open for many other clients besides your organization. They control how they carry out their work and they cannot be expected to work on a regular basis for your organization.

Even beyond the legality issue, hiring someone on contract sends them the signal that they are not part of the organization. Only use contractors for occasional, short-term specialty jobs. Note that if any of these contractors do not have their own registered business, you will have to report what you paid them to your government. In the United States, if you pay a non-employee who does not own a registered business more than 600 dollars, you will need to submit form 1099 to the IRS and send a copy to the contractor.

6.2 Purpose (Mission) Remedies

If you checked any of the boxes under the Purpose Ailments category in the diagnostic chapter, your organization's mission statement needs some adjustments. Either it is not doing its job or the purpose is being presented improperly. Because your mission statement is the skeleton of your organization it supports and reaches to every thing you do. Common flaws include a mission statement that is too long (more than one sentence) or vague or one that is redundant to other organizations in the area.

Your mission statement needs to clearly state what your organization is meant to do, where it does it, and for whom. Here's an example of a mission that is too vague and likely redundant to others: Helping the children. An upgrade could result in: Offering afterschool activities to children ages five to twelve in Maplewood, North Dakota.

It's time for a rewrite when a mission statement is doing a lousy job explaining the organization's reason for existence. Only the leaders of an organization should have the authority to change the mission statement, so if you are an outsider, you can only suggest this to them.

Changing a mission statement is a very difficult process. It should be. Otherwise anyone could change them and send organizations into tailspins whenever they wanted. Before all of you jump into the task, look back at how your current mission statement was created. Respect that process. Note who was involved and any records of the process. Healthy organizations always hold fast to their roots, including the passion of the people who founded them. This history feeds the passion of current leaders and inspires new helpers to offer their time. Retain some wording from that original mission statement that carries the passion of your founders.

The process of rewriting a mission statement (also for writing the original for a brand new organization) will span several days of intense, productive discussions among the leaders of the organization. Start broad, looking at the entire organization. You will have an advantage over founders of a brand new organization because you will have seen your organization in action. What about it makes people cheer and offer to help? Which characteristics cause people to respond negatively? Do you want to embellish or abolish any of these?

You might find that your current mission statement is redundant to another organization serving your community. This will lead to a much more complex remedy. Redundant organizations are founded for various reasons, most falling into two categories—factions or ignorance. In the case of factions, shunned leaders split off from one organization and found a new, nearly identical organization in retaliation. In the case of ignorance, founders rush in to create an organization without checking for existing organizations already doing that same work. Their time would have been better spent assisting the existing organization. Either way, redundant organizations do tremendous harm by confusing constituents and pulling energy and resources away from their shared cause.

Though you may never know the reason your organization was founded as redundant to another, a thoughtful and sympathetic invitation to meet with the leaders of the other organization is in order. Even in the case of retaliation you can hope that enough time has passed for old wounds to heal. The leaders could offer ways to adjust your mission to compliment rather than replicate their work. A merger is another option, though it rarely works since the organizations who attempt a merger are often hampered by the common dysfunctions you've been reading about in this book. However, if both organizations are healthy (aside from this redundancy) and embrace the idea, merger could be something to look at. Otherwise, take their input very seriously and be sure that your revised mission is clearly distinct from theirs.

As you work with your team to revise your mission statement, be sure to discuss any concerns with people outside the leadership team, especially people you value as partners and supporters. You can make these processes open, such as through public forums, or more intimate through personal meetings with individuals.

However, I caution against inviting outside supporters to the meetings where you actually rewrite the mission statement. People outside of the leadership team will not take the time to examine the entire organization and all of the intricacies that you as leaders must understand before choosing the final words. They aren't responsible for the health and well-being of the organization as you are and so will not give the process the necessary gravity. If you and the others are adamant about including outside participants in the meetings, then limit their involvement to the early meetings and looking at drafts of the revision. Only the leaders should be in attendance at the meeting that finalizes the mission statement.

At the start of these meetings I like to keep things messy. Use lots of big pieces of paper taped to the wall or several white boards. Start broad by discussing the merits of your organization, what it is meant to do, and the culture you expect. Everyone should take their own notes. Give ample time to this discussion, perhaps one or even two hours. Then take a break to allow everyone to process their ideas. When you resume, write out each person's chosen words and phrases in no particular order on the paper or white boards for all to see. Discuss contentious words or phrases. Fill the paper and white boards.

Finish this meeting by narrowing that messy list to the group's preferred words and phrases. One fun method is to give each person three colorful stickers and then ask them to place their stickers next to their favorite words and phrases. They can stick all three next to one or place one each on three different ones. When everyone is finished, the winning words and phrases should be clear. This first meeting can adjourn with the designated note taker recording these winning words and phrases to email to attendees prior to your next meeting. By adjourning at this stage you allow your fellow leaders to process the ideas discussed.

Obviously you'll need at least one more meeting, perhaps more. At the final meeting, start with your original mission statement and review what you learned about the process and passion the founders went through to write it. Remind everyone of these roots and the importance of retaining at least an essence of the original mission to honor its past. Then open the discussion to the new words and phrases and how a revision might look. Remember to keep it to one simple yet clear sentence. Choose words that do the most work capturing the purpose, the culture, where the organization works and for whom, then cut all the rest.

You'll have to fight the temptation to skip this process to

simply rewrite the original mission statement. When your fellow leaders try this, explain that it only wastes time. Until all of you have examined your organization and discussed its merits, you will not have the substance with which to do a proper job.

Approval of the revised mission statement should be by consensus. Consensus does not mean that every leader sees the decision as their best choice. It simply means that every leader's concerns have been included so that all leaders can agree to the final decision. Even if you operate under majority rule, passing a mission statement that some leaders disagree with not only stinks of an unfinished job, it could lead to factions and the crises they cause. Take the time to adjust the words until everyone on the leadership team is happy with it. This needs to include the entire board of directors and, if you have one, your executive director.

Once your revised mission statement has been approved by all leaders, you will have to amend official documents as well as anywhere the old statement was posted including your website, brochures, and promotional materials.

Supposing you have an excellent mission statement, but it's being presented improperly, the remedy is to create what is often called a corporate identity manual. Such a manual includes strict policies on how the organization is to be presented to the public—including its logo, colors, slogan, and mission statement. I'll offer more details about such manuals as well as conducting effective meetings in the next chapter.

6.2.1 Name Change

It's likely that during this process someone will suggest changing the name of the organization. Any time the makeup of an organization is questioned it opens the door to radical overhauls by people new to the organization or outsiders with their own, undeveloped opinions about it. Look out for this from the very start and know that it can be a danger sign. While it is wise to take a serious look at a name that is doing the organization harm, a name change should never be considered lightly. New leaders are especially prone to suggesting a name change when they have had little involvement in the organization.

This isn't to say that random, half-baked opinions about your organization are not valuable. In fact they are useful because they are a snapshot of your public image. But a mission statement should not be rewritten in response to a public image as these are often based on false information and rumors. The same goes for changing the name and demolishing other core structural elements. Unless your organization's name includes offensive language or can be proven to be doing significant harm to your efforts, place cries for a name change in the category of threats. At the very least, such a wanton radical change will sever the organization from all previous branding. Depending on the level of harm the original name was causing, abandoning all your previous promotions and branding might still be worth it. A name change is akin to starting a new organization, so take into account everything you will lose in this process as well as the dangers you will be inviting. At best it will be like starting over—not so serious for a young organization, but very damaging for one with more than five years of history. At the worst, it will open the door to a faction taking control of the organization—a full-blown crisis.

Take a deep breath as you resolve to remedy your purpose ailments. Revising a mission statement is an enormous amount of work, but every minute will be worth it if your organization's current skeleton is not offering the structure that is needed.

6.3 Public Image Remedies

Great organizations working for significant social change always have opponents. This is not a bad thing, even as you hope they will change their minds someday. Public image ailments occur when people you'd expect to support and tap into your work are repelled. Sometimes this is self-inflicted when leaders disseminate an image they believe fits their intent even as it undermines their reputation. Other times, people outside of the organization spread warped rumors. Either way, you and your fellow leaders will have to reverse the damage.

The very first step is self-examination. This can be difficult, especially with leaders who have nurtured their organization from its beginning. It's your baby. Who couldn't love your baby? Well, if you're facing public-image ailments, lots of people have fallen out of love with your baby and now you have to figure out why. Look at how you've been presenting the organization. List all of your external communications in the past six months and note whether they were sufficient and included the information you intended. Talk with people you trust who are not involved with your organization and ask them what impression they get when they look at your website, materials, and your most recent communications. Take ample notes and put stars next to any details that are repeated often. Never make drastic changes to your image in response to one or two people. They might blurt out a random comment that they barely gave a moment's thought to. When you find the culprit messages and images, change them immediately.

Next, you have to hunt down any sources of misinformation in the community. Even if you've changed the sources under your control, look for places they may have spread or even mutated. An eager reporter might have read a badly worded e-newsletter you sent out, then inflated that wrong impression into a full-blown newspaper article or blog post. A partner organization might have taken that same negative nugget and added it to their e-newsletter that spread beyond your community. Talk to your active members, volunteers, employees, partners, and anyone who has an ear for hearsay and ask them to help in the search. Request the removal of all improper information about your organization.

Sometimes you will find that damaging messages have settled in and, depending on where they might be posted or repeated, cannot be removed. Your opponents might be having a jolly good time slandering your organization. A self-righteous reporter might see himself as a clever little rabble rouser, especially if the conflict he starts sells more ads. Perhaps another organization is slandering yours to take credit for your work. In such cases, the remedy is actually quite palatable: ramp up your good work and do an extraordinary job of spreading the news about it. After a few months of this your slanderers and libelers will be revealed as bullies trying to undermine an organization that is benefitting the community.

Never respond directly to a slanderer's attack. This is usually what they want and will only encourage them. Don't stoop to their level. Also realize that legal action is rarely successful. Only in the most extreme cases, when you can prove slander or libel has caused your organization measurable harm, will you stand to gain a small restitution, and this after years of court battles. Your energy will be far better spent increasing your organization's good work and promoting it. Then continue these positive external messages so that slanderers will only look silly making their false claims.

Now let's take an in-depth look at the policies and procedures that can serve as your organization's safety net whenever trouble brews.

Chapter 7
Policies and Procedures Remedies

Without proper policies in place many ailments can spiral out of control. In this chapter I will present common policies known to keep problems in check. Don't get hung up on the formats I recommend. Instead, contemplate the reasons for these policies and the predicaments they are designed to prevent, then adapt them to your needs.

Healthy organizations create a culture in which everyone is expected to work together toward the mission. Because this team effort prevents ailments, leaders of such organizations rarely have to refer to written policies and procedures. But having them in place in case calamity does strike creates a vital safety net that no organization can do without.

Proper procedures do wonders for discouraging bad behaviors. Policies set a culture of kindness and respect into writing and serve as the backup that leaders need when such a culture is challenged. But policies cannot create such a culture. Only the leaders can by following their agreed-upon procedures and upholding the principles set out in their policies.

I was once told about a board chair who became intoxicated by his power, threatening staff and board members with dismissal if they did not follow his wishes. Each of the board members he tried to manipulate looked him in the eye, one-on-one in different settings, and told him their organization didn't treat people that way. None of them were aware that he had threatened the others and none of them referred to policies. They simply knew that his behavior was inappropriate and told him so. It wasn't long before that chair stepped down. I heard this story from one of these board members, steeped in pride. What saved them from a crisis was the culture they had nurtured together over the years. It may have been written into their policies, but they tapped it from their hearts.

Sometimes situations slip past the strongest cultures and descend into the danger zone. That's when you'll need strong policies as your safety net. Establish them in good times because you cannot create sound policies in the midst of a crisis. Even though this work might seem boring and unnecessary at the moment, get it done before problems strike.

Everyone on your leadership team should be actively involved in creating and upgrading your policies. Their involvement will not only ensure their input is included, it will instill a sense of ownership. This in turn will motivate them to abide by and uphold these policies.

7.1 Productive Meetings

Productivity is important for all meetings, including when you sit down together to create policies and procedures. Productive meetings keep leaders energized and focused on activities that produce results. Meetings like this are fun, especially for people who enjoy leadership.

Unless this is an emergency, the first step toward a productive meeting takes place at least five days beforehand when a leader sends a *draft* agenda to all the other leaders and asks for their input. Set a deadline at least two days prior to the meeting for agenda changes and new agenda items to be proposed to the leader who sent out the draft. This leader can make simple changes and additions. If significant agenda changes are needed, this two-day window allows a revised draft to be sent around for comment and input. Preparing an agenda this way restricts random topics being brought up during the meeting. By having a clear and agreed-upon system for changing the agenda well before the meeting, all leaders will be comfortable sticking to the agenda, which will move discussions along toward an on-time adjournment.

Start initial meetings by agreeing on meeting rules. Ask the others to suggest rules that will ensure you all reach your intended meeting goals, and write these on a flip chart or white board for all to see. This gives each leader a chance to offer rules discouraging behaviors that have disturbed them in past meetings. Common meeting rules include:

- Only one person speaks at a time.
- Each agenda item must end with a decision or a defined action along with the name of the person responsible for completing it.
- All cell phones must be turned off.
- A time keeper is designated to ensure the meeting finishes on time.
- And so on...

This process should take no more than five minutes. Post the list in easy sight of all attendees to point to in case the meeting spins out of control. Then designate these rules for all future meetings.

Some organizations either choose to or are required to follow established meeting procedures such as Robert's Rules of Order. Because they have no connection to your unique organization's needs, such rules should only be considered in addition to your agreed-upon meeting rules, if at all. I generally recommend against such cut-and-paste, impersonal meeting rules because attendees have no ownership in them and they tend to hinder useful discussion.

Always assign a note taker at the very start of each meeting. This is often the secretary of the board, but does not have to be. Very new organizations may not have established titles for their board members. Other times the secretary might be unable to take the notes and can receive them from the note taker in draft form after the meeting.

Leadership meetings can cover lots of territory very quickly. Unless someone is taking notes, great ideas will be lost. Not only are such losses a shame for the organization, they can also cause resentment in leaders who believe they were ignored. Usually the loss of great ideas is not intentional, but to a budding leader, it can appear that the others regard their ideas as less important than their own. Avoid this potential rupture in your team by designating a note taker who can capture everyone's ideas, along with the decided actions, and set the names of those responsible next to each action item. Soon after the meeting, this note taker sends them around as a draft for everyone to offer needed changes. Prior to or at the next meeting, all of you should approve these draft minutes at which point they will become the official minutes for your files. Meeting minutes are a permanent record of when decisions were made. They also document your professional conduct in case anyone questions your activities.

Do your best to keep your ongoing meetings to one hour. This is especially important for boards of directors who meet monthly, because the people you will want on your board will generally not tolerate longer meetings at this frequency. You can achieve this by sending all reports and update information prior to the meeting date, leaving the meeting time to discussion.

7.2 Bylaws

Bylaws are internal policies that you and future leaders refer to for leadership procedures. In order for your bylaws to serve this purpose, they must be as short and concise as possible—two to four pages is plenty—and use common language that all future leaders will clearly understand. Leave out more specific policies such as meeting rules, employee expectations, and office systems used in daily operations that require frequent updates.

Role confusion or board and committee dysfunction can signal a need for a bylaws revision. In case you have also identified purpose ailments, consider combining these revision efforts since your mission statement is the crown jewel of your bylaws. Bylaws revisions must be rare and follow a similar, comprehensive process because this document affects the structure of the organization.

Some organizations use their incorporation document (called Articles of Incorporation in the U.S.) as their bylaws, but I do not recommend this. Such documents are convoluted, focused on financial conflicts of interest and operation details that qualify the organization for national nonprofit status. Very little of their content serves as leadership guidance.

Beware of nonprofit bylaws templates that circulate on the internet and through lazy nonprofit coaches. Many of these templates include clauses that will eventually pit leader against leader. Most are also overburdened with legal language that is indecipherable even by an attorney. Your bylaws will be unique, designed to guide your organization through leadership changes and decision making based on your specific culture and needs. Cut-and-paste bylaws language cannot do that.

Next is a very simple worksheet that demonstrates how straightforward your bylaws can be. If you like, you can simply replace my text with your bylaws language. Your final document should not be much longer than what I have written.

BYLAWS OF (ORGANIZATION'S NAME)
Article I: Purpose
Insert your mission statement here.
Article 2: Members
Clearly state whether or not your organization has members and what privileges they have. If you give your members voting rights, include safeguards designed to prevent a takeover by self-serving individuals.
Article 3: Board of Directors and Executive Director
Describe how leaders are chosen and any requirements they must meet before being invited to that position. I recommend requiring a minimum amount of active involvement with your organization before someone can be considered for the board. This will ensure that your new board members at least understand the

purpose and culture of your organization.

I do not recommend member-elected boards because the vast majority of members will not investigate nominees before casting their vote. This allows self-serving people to take over the organization for their personal goals. I realize that in some countries, members are required to vote for board members. If this is the case in your country, you can avoid danger by including in your bylaws very strict criteria for board nominees such as significant time spent volunteering for the organization, three or more recommendations from current partners, and similar.

Specify the duties for each title. Clearly differentiate between the roles of board members (broad, governance level) and the executive director (in charge of day-to-day operations). Designate a minimum and maximum number of board members. I recommend no fewer than three and no more than twelve. This will ensure enough hearts and minds for great ideas and avert the apathy that results from too large a board. If you choose to include term limits for board members, be sure to find a means of welcoming these informed and committed leaders to stay involved. I recommend that you make your executive director a voting member of the board. This bridges the divide between staff and board and results in a more egalitarian organization.

Require that all decisions that impact the organization be made by the entire board to prohibit committees from making such decisions. You can also add a clause that states that committees can only bring their recommendations to the full board and are never given decision-making power.

Include a paragraph on removal that clearly states that significant, proven harm to the organization must have been committed by that leader (board member or executive director) and that a full consensus of the entire board is required. If you and your team prefer majority vote, then removal of any leader must be by super majority—at least two thirds if not three quarters of the entire board. Allow an easier removal process for inactive board members, because you do not want uninformed people making decisions for the organization. This can include missing two consecutive board meetings and a warning process that removes them from decision making until they catch up on all vital information. Specify a catch-up period in which an absentee board member may re-engage and state that if they do not, they will simply be removed from the board.

Include a paragraph for resignation. Usually all that is required is notice in writing from that leader to any member of the board or a specific board member.

Article 4: Amendments

Changing your bylaws must be a serious and arduous process, otherwise random amendments could easily derail the organization. Clearly state that any amendment to these bylaws requires a full consensus of the entire board. If you and your team prefer majority vote, then all amendments must be approved by super majority of at least two thirds if not three quarters of the entire board. This should prevent overzealous leaders pushing through unnecessary and harmful amendments.

Your country might require other specifics, so include those in their appropriate spot. At the bottom of your bylaws document include a note stating the date the Board of Directors approved them.

7.3 Annual Planning

Planning is the most important responsibility for you and your fellow leaders because no one else will do it. Without a plan, you will waste enormous amounts of time and money dabbling in random activities and will likely lose many potential leaders and helpers along the way. No one stays around long without an effective plan.

There are two types of planning you as leaders have to engage in: long-term planning and annual planning. Briefly, long-term planning creates a clear picture well into the future, including what your community will look like after your work is done. Your mission statement drives all of it. You will read more about long-term planning later.

Annual planning, as the name implies, takes place every year and maps out specific activities toward your long-term goals. Near the end of each year at a special meeting, at least half a day long, you and your fellow leaders will examine your expectations for the past year compared to what actually happened. Using this reality check, you will work together to develop your work plan and budget for the coming year. Reference your long-term plan to ensure that the details you outline for the year will follow the shortest and most effective path toward your mission and general goals.

Choose either a calendar year or a different fiscal year. Most organizations operate under a calendar year that starts January 1 and ends December 31. Others choose to start July 1 and end June 30 or start October 1 and end September 30. There are various reasons for choosing such odd fiscal years, usually to align with similar organizations. For instance, many local governments in the United States use the July to June year. Unless there is an important reason to do otherwise, I recommend you stick with the calendar year because it is the most common and all your team members will easily remember the expected start and finish of your budget cycle. Also, members and donors will understand what time frame you are referring to in your annual reports.

Your annual work plan/budget should be short enough (two to three pages is ideal) that all leaders and key staff of the organization can easily check progress. It should be referenced at every board meeting and will become your basis for funding proposals. Prohibit jargon. Use common language and choose only words that bring clear meaning. Delete the rest.

Note that I do not separate work plan and budget. While combining them into one document is ideal, they could be in two as long as they are inseparably linked, each section and line dependent on the others. Even the development discussions should flow between work (activities you'll undertake) and the money necessary to make that work possible. I can't count the number of times I've discovered separate work plans and budgets as the cause of organization chaos. It's too easy to outline wonderful tasks for your organization without considering their cost or where the funding will come from. On the other side, it's too easy to blindly set numbers into an income/expense spreadsheet without having to dissect each planned activity for its cost and income potential. Combining and aligning the two is certainly more work, but you will end up with a document that is based on reality and a quality tool for success.

So what is a budget? Most importantly, it is only a projection. However, it is a concise projection that has to come close to reality in order for it to be useful. It should have two sections—income and expense—and either be "balanced," which means the income and expense totals are the same number, or strive for an income surplus. I recommend planning for a budget surplus. When a potential funder or partner verbally asks for your organization's budget, chances are they are simply asking for the expense total because that is what you plan to spend that year.

An organization's first few budgets are often a bit off. Sometimes leaders will shoot too high, expecting everyone who's excited about their new organization to contribute or that most of the grants they apply for will come in. Other leadership teams shoot too low and when unexpected funding comes in, they have to scramble to plan for its appropriate expenditure. Set a policy for adjusting your budget that makes the process a bit difficult to prevent constant changes and the resulting confusion. Schedule at least one budget review and adjustment process halfway through the year to ensure that the document continues to align with reality.

I recommend having three programs and/or projects underway at all times, including at least one that inspires new people to engage with your organization. The other two can be a bit boring, for instance building an interactive program into your website to engage your clients. Such a backstage project can attract funding, pay for staff, and result in a great product, but during the process there is no chance for inspiration.

I caution against taking on more than three programs or projects at any one time. This goes for even the largest organizations. Small organizations should have just three easily managed projects and/or programs. Large organization can take on three larger, more complex efforts. This way your team and supporters will understand what you are doing to achieve your mission. More than three will diffuse energy and pull people in too many directions.

As I noted earlier, even with more than three activities underway, try to fit them into three program categories. If they don't fit into three, your organization is likely taking on too many and too varied activities. Ongoing administrative activities like partner development, fundraising, and office support do not function as programs because they do not cause progress toward the organization's mission, and so need not fit into these three program categories.

Next I will offer a simple example of a Work Plan/Budget for a young organization. Don't get stuck on any of its line items or amounts. It's only meant as a visual example of what a work plan/budget could look like. You and your team will likely create a much different document and can even choose a different format that better fits your needs. But do keep your work plan and budget interconnected and take the time to examine every activity you plan in order to capture every cost and income potential.

INCOME

Supporters	$20,000
Sponsors	$10,000
Grants	$50,000
Sales	$10,000
Service fees	$4,000
TOTAL:	$94,000

EXPENSE

Payroll	$45,000
Payroll expense	$15,000
Health insurance	$6,000
Program 1 expenses	$15,000
Program 2 expenses	$2,000
Program 3 expenses	$2,000
Utilities	$1,500
Website	$500
Printing	$1,000
Postage & Shipping	$500
Phone	$650
Supplies & Services	$750
Transportation	$500
Fees & Dues	$200
TOTAL:	$90,600 (leaving $3,400 as

contingency or surplus for next year)

PROGRAM 1
Include staffing, supplies, promotions, and other operations needed to achieve the program goals for the year.

PROGRAM 2
Include staffing, supplies, promotions, and other operations needed to achieve the program goals for the year.

PROGRAM 3
Include staffing, supplies, promotions, and other operations needed to achieve the program goals for the year.

ADMINISTRATION
Include management staff and associated costs, insurance, contracting with experts, website, and bookkeeping.

FUNDRAISING & PROMOTION
Include mailings, social and fundraising events, grant writing, writing press releases, and other fundraising and promotions activities.

Adjust the budget line items to include all expenses identified in each work-plan section. Include all administrative costs beyond salaries such as insurance, supplies, and office infrastructure needed to carry out all the day-to-day activities. Avoid too many earmarked funding sources such as project-specific grants that often do not cover these overhead expenses. Include several income sources from individuals such as your members, donors, and customers because this funding is not earmarked. Once you and your fellow leaders are happy with your work plan/budget, note this approval in your meeting minutes and include a note on the actual document that reads: Approved by Board of Directors (date).

A cash-flow chart is a useful additional tool for tracking your progress throughout the year and ensuring you spend only money that is available. Your cash-flow chart will work best in a spreadsheet with columns per month. You can add rows to break out each budget item into specifics. For instance, "payroll" can be broken into separate rows for each staff member. You might also want to break out parts of each program. Find an example of a cash-flow spreadsheet complete with calculating formulas on One Street's website under Management in the left menu.

7.4 Corporate Identity Manual
A corporate identity manual controls the branding of your organization and inhibits the misuse of your organization's mission statement, name, logo, colors, messaging, and any other part of its image. Before you start on this manual, all of these elements should be in place. We've already discussed how to create a strong mission statement along with an appropriate name. If you and your team have not settled on a logo, colors, or messaging, start with a

committee that includes at least one expert in these areas to ensure quality results. Once all branding elements are in place, engage all leaders in the development of this manual so they will uphold it.

Misuse can come in enticing forms such as another organization or company using your name and logo for a fundraising raffle. On the surface, this can appear to be a nice idea, an easy way to bring in money. But further investigation usually reveals that most of the money and all the goodwill will remain with the raffle group. Keep a wary eye out for misuse and include language in your manual to counteract it.

Include in this manual the exact dimensions of your organization's logo, the exact brand colors using common color codes such as the Pantone Matching System (PMS) or CMYK, the exact wording of your tagline or slogan, and rules for the use of all of these components.

In addition, I recommend that you include the designation of one spokesperson to ensure that all of your external communications are correct and consistent. Don't include their name, since you shouldn't have to update your manual every time a new person takes this post. Do include their title. For instance, the executive director would be a good choice for a small to mid-sized organization; the public relations director could be a good fit for a large organization. Specify their responsibilities such as checking every press release and e-newsletter prior to sending and developing relationships with media representatives. All inquiries from media representatives should be referred to your spokesperson.

In just a few pages, great corporate identity manuals clearly lay out these details. Search the internet for "corporate identity manual" to find countless examples.

7.5 Executive Director and Employee Policies

Policies that offer guidance for your executive director and employees provide essential stability. By articulating expectations, they ensure that hard workers are rewarded and slackers are confronted fairly. Without these policies, your employees will not have the confidence to fully commit to their job. From the other side, new or overzealous board members will be tempted to fire these people on a whim and there will be no way of stopping this.

Include your executive director in your bylaws as one of your organization's leaders with an equal level of responsibility with your board members. I also recommend making them a voting member of the board. Proper procedure for firing your executive director should be found in only one place: the "Removals" section of your bylaws, including proof of harm and agreement by the full board of directors before any leader can be removed. This fair and respectful treatment will give your executive director the confidence to do a good job.

Job descriptions and agreements are important for all of your employees, including your executive director. A job description outlines the required duties without getting into daily tasks. It can be used in the job announcement you send out, then be included in the employee's agreement once they start. An employee agreement should also include salary, expected hours per week (or simply full-time for an exempt employee), benefits, pay period, and supervisor. A clear job description, agreed to by the employee before the first day on the job, gives supervisors what they need to point to when a warning is necessary.

Always pay your employees a market rate for similar positions in your area. This shows that you value their role in your organization. On a more practical level, it will prevent them from taking another job only because they need more money. Keeping your best employees will save your organization untold costs in retraining replacements. This is all the more vital for your executive director because once you find a great fit for this top staff position, you do not want them moving on simply because their salary is too low. Your executive director will be part of the budget discussion and, while they will appreciate all of you setting their salary at an appropriate level, they must also agree to the work needed to bring in that funding.

As I emphasized earlier, never include a time limit in your executive director's agreement or any suggestion of this such as their having to pass an annual review in order to continue in the job. Such time limits strip any confidence they could have in their job and will encourage them to look for another employer who has more faith in them. If you and your fellow leaders are not fully confident with hiring a particular person as executive director, create a trial period such as their first six months on the job. Give them a different title like interim director with its own agreement. Outline exact goals they must achieve within that period. If they come through that trial period having done a good job, replace it with an ongoing executive director agreement that is backed up by your bylaws. Otherwise they need to move on.

Integrate ongoing review of all employees into daily procedures and leave out annual reviews. If any employee is underperforming or does something wrong, they need to sit down with their supervisor immediately (in the executive director's case, this is the entire board of directors) to work out a solution and make necessary changes. Such meetings are the place for warnings, also delivered in writing, that lead to appropriate firings. Annual reviews do not work in any of these regards. They tempt supervisors to put off difficult discussions and warnings until the end of the year or force unnecessary stress on employees who are actually doing a good job.

Employees who are proud to work for you will stay on the job for many years. Once they are ready to move on, they will be eager to record their job duties, achievements, and lessons learned in order to help their replacement start where they left off.

An employee manual supplements individual employee agreements. Such a manual is generally ten to twenty pages packed with useful information for incoming employees. Such a manual can start with your organization's mission and a description of the culture and principles all of you abide by. Details can include offenses that will not be tolerated such as harassing other employees or being intoxicated on the job. By designating these in a manual that new employees are required to read, a supervisor will have the backup they need to fire someone for extremely harmful behavior without having to give them a warning. An employee manual can outline expectations for professional dress as well as upkeep of the office, how to work with volunteers, who to go to for particular problems, how to purchase supplies, various roles of leaders and employees, holidays, and how to deal with vacation or sick days, and many other operational details. Such a manual will prevent common misunderstandings and will add to the confidence of your employees so they can focus on their job.

Find examples of job descriptions, agreements, and employee manuals on One Street's web site under Management in the left menu.

Pay attention to the titles you give to people. A director is always at the management level. As noted already, the executive director manages the entire organization. But lower director positions are also management level, such as your program director or director of finance, and can also be called managers, i.e., program manager. These positions come with leadership expectations. They will have staff members and volunteers who answer to them and they will take on much greater responsibilities for either the entire organization or the department they are in charge of. These are generally full-time salaried, exempt positions, not hourly. When hiring for a director-level position, look for prior leadership and management experience. It is best to hire people who have already been actively involved in your organization.

Lower, less responsible positions come with titles such as coordinator, assistant, administrator, and associate. Do not give such titles to anyone in a management role. Someone hired as a coordinator should never be expected to perform leadership duties. On the flip side, someone hired to perform basic administrative or program duties should never be given a director or manager title. Inappropriate titles will tempt inexperienced employees to override leadership decisions or will undermine the authority of those who do have management duties.

7.6 Member, Donor, and Volunteer Systems

Regard your members, donors, and volunteers as precious to your organization. They will always be the best sources for anything you and your fellow leaders need. If you have a job opening, send it to this list of fans hoping they will apply, and ask them to spread it. If you need a donation for a piece of office equipment, include this in the e-newsletters you send them. If a volunteer does a great job designing an event flyer, they might like to design your new brochure. This list of folks is also your best place to look for leadership talent for new board members because they are already actively engaged with your organization.

In order to attract these precious helpers, set in place a comprehensive system that invites and encourages new people to get involved. Anyone who has any interest in your organization should want to be a member (or supporter if you don't have members). Not only that, all of your members should be so proud of their membership that they will encourage others to join. When you are asked by a stranger whether you are a member of your organization you will know your network has reached well beyond your small group of friends and acquaintances. There is no single mechanism for creating such a magnetic culture. Do everything you can to spread a message that everyone is welcome to take part in your work. They can join as members to add themselves to the strength of your organization. They can donate money beyond membership dues to help pay the costs of your work. And they can offer their time and skills as volunteers. State this on your website and in printed materials. Coach your board members, staff, and volunteers to spread this message and invite everyone who might like to help.

Develop a volunteer system that specifies jobs that are suited to volunteers and always have these ready when new volunteers show up. Avoid assigning anything critical to a volunteer because they will often not complete the job. This could cause your organization harm and make them feel bad for letting you down. Give them basic jobs that allow partial completion so their contribution is sure to be beneficial. Preparing mailings, creating event decorations, and painting rally signs are all good examples. For your volunteers who are expert in certain areas, give them very specific, small bites of each job you need done so that if they leave early, at least they will have completed a finite part of the effort. Always assign a staff or board member to oversee the work of volunteers to ensure they stay on task.

Create a means of recording people's assistance, whether it be money or time. A small organization can do this well with a simple spreadsheet. Larger organizations that expect thousands of helpers may want to invest in software specifically designed for donor and volunteer tracking. Contact information is critical so you can thank them, send them news updates, and ask them to assist again. Include separate columns for first and last name and each section of the mailing address. This makes it easy to search as well as transfer into a label-making file for mailings.

Put one person in charge of recording and following up on all contributions. Have this person send out a thank you letter immediately following any contribution. Work with this person to write down all the procedural details that make this system function smoothly. This document will guide people who take on this job in the future.

7.7 Operations and Bookkeeping

Your operations systems can include your office, its furniture, your computers, and any devices you use to carry out your programs. Antique computers are often blamed for bad morale, but don't overlook more ordinary things such as the chairs your employees have to sit in all day. A small investment in better computers, phones, or office chairs (or a call for such donations) can go a long way toward improving how people feel about their job. This will show through their interactions with your members, partners, and clients and will increase their productivity.

Bookkeeping is just one of your operations systems. By understanding your books, you and your team can make those fine adjustments that spell the difference between budget surplus and shortfall. Also, because it captures all financial activity, good bookkeeping wards off the temptation to steal.

Bookkeeping and accounting are different though related. Bookkeeping is the act of recording all income and expenses. This is the responsibility of the leaders and managers. I do not recommend hiring an outside bookkeeper. Anyone who does the books for your organization will have the opportunity to embezzle money, but outside contractors have fewer ties to your organization than staff members. Even if a manager does the books each day, check their work and ensure that deposits into your organization's bank account match income.

Accounting organizes the information captured through bookkeeping into useful reports that meet tax reporting requirements. You will likely need an accountant's help with payroll and year-end tax preparation.

Before hiring an accountant, ensure you are comfortable working with them and that they can translate accounting lingo into everyday language. The best accountant in the world would be useless if the way they explain your books sounds like a foreign language. Your accountant can help set up your bookkeeping and accounting system and decipher the information it reveals.

For organizations in the United States, I recommend using QuickBooks for your bookkeeping and accounting software because it is commonly used by accountants. If you are elsewhere, ask accountants in your area which accounting software they'd recommend.

If you can't afford a nice accounting program like QuickBooks right away, a budget/actual cash flow chart in a spreadsheet such as Excel or the free version from OpenOffice will suffice until you can. In the United States, there are several software sellers that offer deep discounts on QuickBooks for 501(c)(3) nonprofits. Start by checking Techsoup.org. If that doesn't work, do an internet search for nonprofit software discounts.

Work with your accountant to determine which line items to include in your income and expense sections of your software or spreadsheet. Include just enough to cover all your common income categories and expense items. Too many or too few will make your reports impossible to decipher. By creating a quality system from the start, you will save significant time in the future.

Record all of your expenses in your organization's check register and balance it each month with your bank statement. The best way to do this is to pay bills and buy supplies with checks. A debit card can work, but a check will give you more information if you have to look up the expense later. Avoid using credit cards because they will tempt you to spend money your organization does not have. Plan ahead instead. Plus fees and interest are higher on business credit cards than on personal ones and can siphon outrageous amounts of money. Also avoid auto-bill-paying services because you will lose control of your expenses and miss recording them promptly. Never pay bills or buy major supplies with cash because you won't have a backup record of the expense. Set up a petty cash system in your office for staff to purchase small supplies, then record these receipts promptly.

Keep all your records, bank statements, and receipts as long as you have room to store them. If you must throw some away, note that U.S. laws require that you keep your bank statements and receipts for a minimum of three years. Even after three years, never throw away your organization's bookkeeping records or tax paperwork.

Once your bookkeeping and accounting system is set up and you've gotten into the swing of it you'll find it is not as difficult as it might seem now. All it requires is an accurate way to record every transaction of your organization on both the income and expense side, then arrange these numbers to allow anyone to see a clear picture of how you are doing.

Filing your organization's taxes each year is a requirement whether you have a superb accounting system or not. You will have to have accurate bookkeeping in order to file the correct

information, but don't put off filing your taxes while you are
setting up this system. Work with your accountant to track down
all the necessary information and get that paperwork in on time.
Otherwise you will face mounting penalties and your nonprofit
status may be jeopardized. There are watchdog groups that note
when organizations miss filing their taxes and their disapproval can
undermine your organization's reputation. If you have missed any
tax deadlines, work with your accountant to remedy this situation
immediately.

Next we'll look at remedies for communication ailments.
Such ailments affect the most vital systems of your organization,
aligning with the respiratory and circulatory systems of the body,
so prepare to implement these remedies as soon as you can.

Chapter 8
Communication Remedies

Communication ailments are always serious. External communications release the story about your work out into the world, much like a respiratory system. When these stop, your organization has stopped breathing. Internal communications send information nutrients to your team, much like a circulatory system. When they stop, your organization is having a heart attack. That's why it's vital to treat even minor communication ailments before they reach a crisis level.

8.1 External Communication

When external communication ceases and the website has not been updated you can count on your organization's public image plummeting. This usually occurs not from malice or infighting, but because those in charge got distracted from this duty. The website is particularly important because everything should point back to it for further details about your organization. If visitors find that the latest news item on the website is months old, they will likely not return. Schedule regular website updates especially for your home page so returning visitors will see something new each time. This doesn't mean a totally new look. The framework, color scheme, and logo need to remain for proper branding. Inserting a latest news section that can easily be updated is all you need to keep it looking fresh. Also remove any dated items or move them to an archived section, otherwise anything with an old date will signal abandonment to visitors.

External communication ailments often include inconsistency in branding such as different logos and colors in postings and materials. Set in place systems that prevent this and ensure that one person is held responsible for ongoing, professional, and appropriate external communication. Your corporate identity manual is the best place to capture these policies.

Institute a constant flow of pertinent communication to your supporters and media at a rate that reminds, but does not annoy. Use e-newsletters, blog posts, social media, press releases, responses to like-minded online forums, and so on. By providing this constant flow of accurate and interesting information, you will stay one step ahead of any misinformation being spread.

Communications that are buried in unnecessary information might as well not have been sent. People see this fluff and move on to something else. Expectations for communication have been reduced to meager character counts, so leaders have to cut the fat if they expect their messages to reach their audiences. Leave out the long introductions and sausage making. Start with an exciting hook about a victory or someone whose life was changed by your work. Keep it real, but make it exciting and interesting. Add eye-catching images whenever you can.

Beneficial external communications follow accomplishments. With three interesting programs in full swing this should be no problem. Major accomplishments like the passage or repeal of a law should be sent via press release and repeated

In a violent family everyone could be a victim

through all of your other communication channels. The hiring of a new staff member or announcement of a social gathering for members should use mechanisms like your e-newsletter and social media that go to the appropriate people. Record all of these communications, the people they went to, and the length of time between them.

Active members and volunteers might like to hear from you as much as weekly. Major donors generally need only a monthly e-newsletter and a personal connection with someone from your team a few times a year. Your favorite news reporters may only need a prompt every six months. While you don't want to annoy any of them, neither should you let any of your supporters, partners, or media contacts forget about your organization. You want them to think of your organization first, as the authority for your cause.

Even as you institute this expectation of ongoing external communication, never allow the theft of another organization's work, even the slightest insinuation that your organization was responsible for something you did not do. Also ban jargon that sends a message to potential new helpers that they are not welcome: "If you don't understand this word, you are not allowed in the club." These are early signs of red giant behavior, which I described in Chapter 1. It can gain momentum quickly so stop it in its tracks right away.

There are many variations of false representation. In all such cases, the remedy is to admit you did wrong and apologize. The longer you wait to do this, the farther your organization's reputation will sink and the harder it will be to repair. No official will risk their career supporting the initiatives of an organization with a bad reputation. Potential funders, members, and partners will avoid your organization. Communicate your sincere apology immediately and set in place systems that prevent such destructive actions in the future, including designating just one spokesperson in charge of external communication.

8.2 Internal Communication

Internal communications have to be just as interesting and to the point as what you send out to your supporters and fans. Don't make your board members slog through unnecessary details before reaching the information they need to make important decisions for the organization. Make your staff updates similarly concise.

This concern extends to your board meetings as well. They should be frequent enough to engage the board in overarching decisions as programs and activities move forward. For a very active organization, once a month will keep everyone on top of evolving forces. For a less active, perhaps a more research oriented or think tank sort of organization, quarterly meetings will work fine. Any fewer than quarterly and you will run the risk of your board members dismissing their duties and forgetting the necessary details they need to make informed decisions.

8.2.1 One-Hour Board Meetings

When background information and the draft agenda are sent at least five days prior to each board meeting there is no beneficial reason for the meeting to last more than an hour. Board members who arrive at meetings fully updated will be more attentive and able to participate in discussions. By providing this information early, you do not have to cover it in the meeting. The meeting can then focus on informed discussion followed by the necessary governance decisions outlined in the agenda. The only reason for a board meeting is to engage leaders in discussion and decision making. Remove all other time-wasters.

I highly recommend against board meetings that last more than one hour. There are exceptions, such as national or international organizations that require board members to travel to the meeting, in which case meetings should be less frequent and last longer. But most organizations are locally based so that monthly, one-hour board meetings are sufficient to take care of governance. People you most want on your board, people with governance and management experience, are busy people and are used to meetings lasting no more than one hour. Letting your board meetings drag on will lose these people.

If you find that even after sending all updates and background information prior to meetings you still need to meet for more than one hour, you're likely looking at one of two problems. Either you have not set into place proper meeting rules (covered in the previous chapter) or you are not meeting frequently enough. Even for national and international organizations, I still recommend one-hour phone or Skype conference calls for most of your meetings and perhaps a few day-long, in-person meetings each year. These longer gatherings can have a fun, social element afterward to make the travel worthwhile and build your team spirit.

There's a chance that you will still find your board meetings dragging on past that magical one-hour mark. Take note of why this might be happening. Are board members socializing or discussing details that are not on the agenda? This could signal a need for more committee work in a casual setting to allow these passionate board members to pursue particular activities and investigate new ideas in a smaller, more sociable group. Ask the most talkative if creating a committee would take care of their needs. If the distractions and discussion detours are purely social and amusing, consider adding an optional, fun gathering after each board meeting. After the agenda topics are finished, adjourn the meeting and head outside for a picnic, bike ride, or a visit to your favorite pub. Once this becomes the norm, board members will be happy to stick to the agenda and keep their jokes and play for the fun time scheduled afterward.

8.2.2 Staff and Volunteer Meetings

Sometimes internal communications become too sparse or inconsistent to provide the details people need to do their job. Whenever communication ceases, internal or external, it will always be replaced by hearsay, rumors, and misinformation. Count on it. Within your organization this can lead to your board members, other volunteers, and employees spreading disturbing rumors or stopping their work all together.

Set in place systems that inform your team about current happenings including regularly scheduled meetings. Your board meetings take care of your board. For employees, I recommend weekly staff meetings. Designate one staff member (or board member if you have no employees) who is in charge of coordinating volunteers. Every time a new crew of volunteers arrives for work, this coordinator should provide all the pertinent information about the latest happenings with the organization as well as the duties they will be asked to perform. Your volunteers will always be your organization's best champions, that is, if they are well informed about what is actually going on. If they are not, just as with everyone else involved, they will fall back on rumors and hearsay and will actively spread these.

Accompany these scheduled meetings with an expectation to always share ideas and inspiration, discuss options, investigate new possibilities, and generally work as a team toward the overall purpose of the organization. Don't let scheduled meetings stifle everyday banter and the offering of new ideas. Prompt and encourage these as they bring life to your shared vision.

8.3 Funding

Funding lies under communication remedies, not only because it fits so well with the circulation/bleeding analogy, but because without communication, you won't get any funding. Consider all of your external communication, in fact, everything you accomplish, as fundraising. I don't mean that you should request funding every time you send out a communication; on the contrary. Most of your external communications should focus on accomplishments, assuring funders that their money is well spent. I've learned over the years that people who give don't usually do so at their first encounter. Most will take plenty of time to watch an organization evolve, size up their accomplishments, and note when people they respect rave about the organization's work. This can happen only if you are communicating your accomplishments.

Funding shortfalls can be distressing. In order to experience a shortfall, you must have set expectations in place. The best form for this is an annual work plan/budget. Some leaders I've worked with believe that if they don't have a budget, they can't be disappointed by shortfalls. Unfortunately, the lack of a budget and work plan also leads to shortfalls in impact because these leaders have no idea what they should be doing toward their mission.

Your annual work plan/budget should project your organization's income and expenses to a very close estimate. With this policy document in place, all leaders can move confidently forward and ensure that all the activities necessary for securing the projected income are accomplished. Leaders of young organizations commonly over-project or under-project, but with each year, this document will become more reliable and thus remedy funding shortfalls.

8.3.1 Members and Dues

One funding source leaders often overlook is their membership. Members expect to pay annual dues. Without annual dues, they will not consider themselves members. Even if you don't call your donors "members," many will want to renew their support annually and will expect a renewal request. This is a point of pride to them. They want to contribute to their organization. If you have members, charge annual dues; no "free memberships."

Not only do they want to contribute, members cost your organization money. You have to record their membership, welcome them, thank them, communicate with them, ask them to renew, then record their renewal; an endless cycle. Charge the right amount. I have found that $25 per year is the absolute minimum to cover these costs. You might have to charge more or less depending on your area of the world. Even if you have volunteers do this work, you still need either an employee or board member overseeing those volunteers to ensure they do the work properly. These people could have spent their time on other activities that would have brought your organization accolades and funding. Don't ignore this cost. Charge enough so all costs of each member are covered. If you can, charge a little bit more so your members can actually contribute to your programs.

Don't think of your members and donors just as money machines. Your list of these wonderful people is the best place to find volunteers, board members, and employees. So this funding is in fact more nutritious than other types of funding.

8.3.2 Funder Abuse

Funder abuse usually results from an overreliance on single-source funding. Some major funders—whether they are a representative of a foundation, corporation, or government agency—develop ruthless characteristics much like assailants in a crisis. They get a taste of the power they have over your organization and begin to abuse it in perverted ways. I've encountered funders who give a large sum to an organization and then demand surprise reports on short notice. Others give verbal approval to a grant proposal, then request ridiculous acrobatics from the organization leaders before they will write the check. Still others, who have funded an organization over several years, begin threatening not to fund again unless the leaders jump through fabricated hoops designed for the enjoyment of the funder.

Such abuses can mutate further when a funder attempts to influence your organization; not just offering advice, but demanding you change the structure of your organization and the work you do before they will continue their support. Get out of such relationships immediately. No matter how large their support may have been, it's not worth sacrificing your organization for any amount of money.

Funder abuse can also be self-inflicted. This happens when a well-meaning funder approaches an organization with a grand idea that has nothing to do with its mission. Perhaps it's an organization that provides meals to hungry families and a funder wants them to build a baseball field behind their building because they believe that sports must accompany nutrition. Another case could be a funder insisting that a low-income elementary school open a medical clinic as an attached wing because they saw a statistic on how few low-income families receive regular checkups. They offer to fund the organization to bring their grand idea to fruition. Baseball fields and medical clinics are both fabulous in their own right, but they would drain the energy from each of these organizations and pull them away from their intended purpose. Do not be tempted into such a catastrophe. As I mentioned earlier, this is called "chasing the money" because it conjures the image of someone running away from where they should be. Never allow desperation for money to compromise your principles or your mission. Instead, adjust the size of your efforts to match realistically projected income.

In the case of a kind but misguided funder, carefully and respectfully explain to them that their project does not fit the work you do. Take the time to explain what you actually do. You never know, they might adapt their idea into something that will in fact contribute to your work so that you can work with them.

Whenever you believe you are being abused by a funder or you have simply realized there will be a funding shortfall, look to your other funding sources and find any that can be ramped up. The sources reliant on many individuals will hold the most potential because their level of success matches the amount of energy you put toward them. If you and your fellow leaders cannot find any way to increase other funding sources, you will have to cut your expenses somewhere. Then make notes for your next work plan/budget process to find ways to avoid this recurring in the coming year.

By now you should have a good idea about what has been ailing your organization and the various ways you and your team can remedy your problems. Now let's shift gears from basic remedies into the enjoyable, healthy habits that prevent ailments in the first place.

Section 3

Getting Healthy

Chapter 9
Rehab

Recovering from a major crisis or even a long-nagging ailment brings welcome relief. Celebrate with your fellow leaders and any others who helped. Even this simple celebration will be a major step toward rehabilitation and eventual health. Just as people are always at the core of crises and ailments, they are also at the core of recovery. People are the substance of organizations. And people are where you will start your rehab efforts.

9.1 Physical and Cultural Rehab

Having survived a crisis, your team will be battered. Once the celebration fades, memories of the trauma will drift back and some of your best will entertain thoughts of stepping down. Just working through simple remedies can wear out your team. This is why, even as everyone is still recovering, you'll want to bring them together to rebuild the organization into a healthy one. They will groan and argue that they need a break, but don't let them off the hook. Remind them that they are the leaders of this organization and the only ones who can pull it out of the danger zone. Until all of you take the time to repair the defects that allowed the ailment in the first place, you will remain teetering on the edge of another calamity.

This series of meetings can fit nicely into your regular board meeting schedule as long as the ailment was minor. You will still need to examine every aspect of your organization together to ensure you have identified any flaws that could pull it down once again. However, if you have just come through a major crisis, I highly recommend organizing much longer meetings, perhaps a board retreat over a weekend that will provide enough time to fully examine the most disturbing discoveries.

Cover every ailment and crisis you overcame and identify its causes. Look for other ways to improve your systems and reenergize your team.

Having just come through a serious ailment, some of your fellow leaders may continue bad behaviors. Leaders in the throes of emergencies are not at their best and are prone to being selfish, disrespectful, and hurtful. Your meetings during this stage will be an excellent proving ground for adjustments. Practice showing appreciation, empathy, respect, and kindness toward each other. If there's a slip, point it out immediately and offer better ways that person might have phrased their statement.

Remind everyone that anger is not appropriate in any meeting. It can help us identify issues we are most passionate about. After that, anger does absolutely no good. Instead, it causes people to say and do hurtful things that can disrupt and eventually shatter your team. Guide them to shift anger into more appropriate emotions before sitting down together to discuss solutions.

Have you noticed symptoms that point to red giant behavior, which I discussed in Chapter 1? Has your organization grown so big that it can no longer give off as much beneficial energy as it is consuming? Are you following in the footsteps of an organization that exhibits this harmful behavior? This will be a difficult discussion because the exclusive nature of red giant organizations can create an enticing bubble where leaders enjoy the company of each other even as they cause harm. Guide your team out of this quagmire by discussing ways to increase your positive impact in your community, giving credit where credit is due, and never stealing others work in order to sustain your organization.

As all of you delve into this important work of rehabilitation, start with the principles behind any changes you discuss. By ensuring that everyone on your team, leaders and staff, fully understands the principle behind a procedure, you will create a team that can adapt to any situation and still achieve intended outcomes.

For instance, during these post-crisis meetings you might all decide that your recent crisis would have been avoided if you'd had a more welcoming volunteer system. Such a system would have brought a constant flow of new helpers and ideas. This would have prevented that one leader taking on too much work, getting burnt out, and then attacking the organization.

Okay, that's a great deductive process and a worthy solution. Then you have to get into the details. Who is going to coordinate all these volunteers? How will you word your call for volunteers? What are the jobs you'll give these newbies that will ensure their success and not do any harm? How will you keep track of their names, contact info, and the jobs they have completed so you can thank them appropriately? A spreadsheet is a good answer for this last question. Here's where you can make the slip. You could assign someone to create a spreadsheet that captures volunteer info, forget the other elements, and completely lose the principle behind why you're doing this—to bring a constant flow of new people into the organization. In this scenario, you end up with a snazzy spreadsheet, but no volunteers and the underlying ailment still lurking, ready to ambush your work once again.

Do your best to match staff and volunteers with appropriate roles. An example of an inappropriate role placement could be someone with excellent people skills who wants to work directly with your clients, but is asked to enter computer data instead. People will often want to take on a different role from those they have held in other organizations. We are complex creatures that shift our shapes depending on the context in which we find ourselves. You might encounter someone who serves on the board of your local animal shelter. Her greatest passion is preventing animal abuse, so she is contributing her leadership skills to that cause. Her favorite hobby is gardening and now that she has found your community garden organization, she wants to help. Do not assume that she wants to serve on the board. Board service is intensive and can jump from boring to traumatic in an instant. She's already contributing in this way to her passion. Make sure to ask her what role she would like to engage in for your organization. It's more likely she will want to take an active volunteer role right down in the dirt of your community gardens.

Another group of wonderful people you should never place on your board are your major funders. All board members should be expected to contribute some funding every year. What I mean are the funders who give so much as to actually influence the direction of the organization. Placing them on the board will tempt them to influence decisions that affect the use of their funding. Not only is this illegal, you should never place good people into a situation that tempts them into corruption. No matter how harmless it might seem, do not place your major funders onto your board of directors.

Pressure to elect major funders to a board can sometimes be extreme, usually from other board members who wrongly believe that having a major funder on the board would benefit the organization. I once had to respond to a major funder who asked me to nominate him for the next board election of an organization I used to lead. I tapped every ounce of diplomacy I had to explain to him that this would not be appropriate. I must have said something right because he let it go and continued to fund the organization. No matter who is pressuring you to do this, treat it like an emerging crisis, because that is what it would become if it went through. Gently guide enthusiastic major donors into a more appropriate role that does not include decision making.

Take the time to learn the desires of new people who want to participate in your work. Match them to tasks they will excel in. Supposing you don't have a job that matches a new helper's desires, see if you can create one. Otherwise, note their skills, keep them on your list of folks who receive regular updates, and call them as soon as an opportunity arises to put them to work in their particular field of expertise.

Besides roles within your organization, also distinguish between your customers and people who want to help. This is a common mix-up, especially with new organizations that are struggling to build even their basic infrastructure. Your customers include anyone who answers your invitation to get services or products from your organization. If yours is a social enterprise, you will have actual products that you are selling. If you are a service organization, you may refer to your customers as clients. They are still customers who come to you because you promised to deliver something they need.

Never promise to deliver products or services you cannot deliver. In case you fail to deliver the product or service you promised to any customer, do not expect them to roll with it. Apologize and find a way to remedy their complaint—return their payment or provide an alternative product in a timely fashion. Leaders of young organizations often complain to me that their customers are complaining. These leaders expect their customers to recognize the arduous effort they are going through. Even though the product or service was inferior, these customers should adore this wonderful organization and, instead of complaining, offer to help. No. Wrong. Customers are customers. They came to you because you promised to provide them with a product or service. Never promote a product or service you cannot deliver. Not only will you lose customers and clients, the main reason for your existence, your organization's reputation will plummet.

I have heard that customers are twelve times more likely to tell their friends about a bad experience than a good one. In my casual observation of customer behavior at my bike shop and with the organizations I've worked for, I'd say this is a mighty close estimate. You can hope your customers will tell everyone when you do a great job for them, but they will always talk about that one slip-up, especially if you do not apologize and remedy their complaint. Once such a complaint spreads throughout your community, your reputation will take years to recover.

Sometimes happy customers will want to take an active role as helpers or donors. Make it easy for them to shift into this different role by having volunteer sign-up and donation forms readily available in paper form and online. Just be sure to keep this distinction between customer and helper, along with your accompanying expectations for each, because most customers will remain customers who simply expect you to deliver what you promised.

I have one more recommendation for physical and cultural rehab before we move on to long-term planning. If you are an outsider and successfully helped your organization through an emergency, you are very likely a great candidate for the board of directors. Board members must take an interest in the entire organization and act promptly whenever it is threatened. You have already demonstrated your ability to do so if you helped pull it through its recent struggle. Your ability to recognize the danger and your commitment to see it through point to excellent leadership qualities that your organization can certainly use. As long as you are not a major funder of your organization, think about asking the leaders if they would consider you for a board position when one becomes available.

9.2 Long-Term Planning

Long-term planning should take place about every three or four years. It can be accomplished through a few special meetings that set aside at least half a day each, allowing all leaders to settle into the discussion and ensure all pertinent ideas are captured. Depending on the sort of ailment you have just come through, now might be a good time for this.

Capture your long-term plans in easy-to-use documents. These can include business plans and massive strategic planning documents, but the most important will be your Mission/Vision/Values/Goals document. In fact, if done well, it can serve as your strategic plan. This two- to three-page document will align all your plans and become your source for consistent messaging that will aid in the branding of your organization. Your mission statement crowns this document, offering guidance on everything you do. The other sections—vision, values and goals—capture other viewpoints of your organization to clarify your long-term expectations for potential funders, partners, and helpers. Make the planning meetings that you and your team use to complete or update this document as laid-back and interactive as the ones you used to create or revise your mission statement.

Mission: One sentence that clearly states your organization's unique purpose, distinguishes it from others, and shows who it serves and where it serves; covered earlier under Purpose (Mission) Remedies.

Vision: One paragraph that describes the community your organization serves after your organization has completed its work. Write it in present tense and an upbeat tone that captures the imagination of all the leaders. For instance, a vision statement for a cancer support organization could start: All cancer patients in Anytown are matched with a caregiver. Following sentences would likely note how their families have received support. Refer to your mission statement for ideas. Be specific. Show all aspects of the results of your success. Your vision statement will act as a beacon even through the toughest times.

Values: A list of three to five guiding principles you all agree are important to the success of your organization. Your values will spring from the uniqueness of the community you serve, your particular backgrounds, and how you all view success. Considering ailments you may have just recovered from, your values could include such things as: Compassion and empathy toward others always come before personal gain. In fact, by revealing the opposite of your values, any crisis will contribute to the development of your values—sort of a silver lining.

Goals: This is the only section of the four that you must update every three years or so. That is because you want to actually achieve your goals and move on to others. The first three sections are worth reviewing at that time, but are meant to offer long-lasting guidance without the need for revision. This section is for three to five general goals that align with the mission and could be achieved within three years. They should not include fine details. The detailed activities needed to achieve these goals, also known as tactics, will be developed during your annual planning. Here's an example of a general goal: Ensure that a majority of the disadvantaged people in our community know about and feel welcome to engage with our organization. Such a general goal would necessitate several activities in your annual work plan/budget such as promotions that reach into distressed neighborhoods, and landscaping or graphics in the front of your community center that make it particularly welcoming to your disadvantaged neighbors. None of these specific tactics belong in your Goals section, but they are perfect for your work plan/budget. At this point don't worry about defining or organizing specific tactics. Just list them separately on a "tactics" sheet for later reference during your annual planning process. Considering that you should have three lively programs underway at all times, develop goals that capture the broad expectations of the programs currently underway.

After completing your initial draft of your Mission/Vision/ Values/Goals document, request input from others who have a keen interest in your organization. These can be potential customers and clients, your experts, your helpers, and even friends and family members who can offer ways to clarify the language and ensure you've covered all the important concepts.

This document is meant to be used by future leaders of your organization. Just because you and your fellow leaders understand it doesn't mean others will. After you've received input, get that thesaurus out to replace any vague words with the words that do the most work capturing what all of you want to say. Once you're all happy with it, formally approve it and add a note "Approved by Board of Directors on (exact date including year)."

The work you and your team do to create your Mission/ Vision/Values/Goals document is strategic planning. Unfortunately, this term has sometimes been hijacked by self-interested individuals, consultants, and abusive funders.

In its malignant form, strategic planning becomes an all-consuming, grueling, overpriced, multi-year process that distracts organizations from their work and can tear a leadership team apart. Nonprofit consultants have raked in unimaginable profits by talking leaders into multi-year strategic planning contracts. Unethical funders have sidelined nonprofits by demanding they engage in extensive strategic planning before they will consider them for funding. And self-interested individuals who want to take control of a nonprofit have learned to demand strategic planning as an easy way to hide their intentions as the process derails the organization.

So, when you hear anyone asking for "strategic planning," listen deeper for their intentions. Chances are they are using the term to describe healthy long-term planning such as what is involved in the creation of your Mission/Vision/Values/Goals document or even a business plan. In fact, if someone requests your strategic plan, these documents are sure to satisfy them. But if someone is asking you and your team to engage in an arduous process that would require hiring a consultant (perhaps themselves) and many months if not a few years to complete, step carefully away from that person and return the discussion to long-term planning in the best interest of your organization.

You and your team are the only people who can do this job. It might take a few weeks or even a few months, including several day-long sessions. Give it the time it needs, but don't let it bring your organization to a standstill.

9.3 Public Image Rehab

Public image rehabilitation will be especially important when the news of an organization's troubles has spread throughout its community. The longer bad news remains the final word, the longer it will take to convince people the organization is healthy once again.

First, confirm that the bad news actually did spread. Sometimes when we are engulfed in calamity it seems that it must be the center of everyone else's attention as well. There is a chance that hardly anyone heard about your troubles. If no one knows or was harmed by them, you would actually cause damage by announcing that your troubles are over. In this case, simply get back to work and engage your positive external communication about your achievements.

However, if you are sure that a response is necessary, start by apologizing to any people or organizations you may have harmed. Take responsibility for your organization's actions and work with the people you harmed to remedy the situation. You and your fellow leaders will have to decide how to go about this. If there are only a few people involved, then a private meeting with them should work well. But if the damage you did affected much of your community, you may have to make a public apology. Use the same news and media channels you would for announcing newsworthy achievements. However, only make your apology public if the damage you did was community-wide.

Following your apologies, assuming any are needed, you can move into honest external communication about what occurred, how all of you remedied it, and your plans for moving forward. Keep this information objective and void of any personal accusations. This is another place where passive voice will come in handy. For instance: "Our organization experienced a theft of a significant amount of money" rather than "Sally Downs stole a significant amount of money." Appropriate places for this are your website, e-newsletter, and at your events. As you announce the full story and open the drama up to discussion and input from your constituents, you will find a healthy and fun way to interact with the people who care about your organization.

You can even tap the crisis to bring energy to your organization. If you craft your story well, including how it occurred and the plan to move past it, chances are that many people will be touched by your struggle and will want to help carry this newly healthy organization into a brighter future. For instance, if a faction of board members attempted to hijack the organization to serve their personal needs, tell the story as objectively as you can—including the cheerful ending where those board members moved on to form their own organization or company that is more suited to their goals. People love drama as long as there is a chance for a happy ending. When they can take part in that happy ending (and continuation), all the better.

There's a good chance that your opponents, and possibly even good folks who don't hear the whole story, will continue to spread false and damaging information about your organization. To prevent these messages from doing harm, ramp up your good work and tap all communication channels to flaunt your achievements for at least a few months after your recovery. Then lock into an ongoing external communication system that keeps the truth about your work in front of your community at all times and thus keeps false rumors from spreading.

9.4 Structure Upgrades

When people inside or outside of the organization have misbehaved or are repelled, there is probably something amiss in the structure. Your mission statement upgrades and long-term planning will remedy the most common structural ailments. Also take an honest look at other needed structural changes. Should your organization shift into a for-profit structure? This would lose all of the goodwill and social networking associated with nonprofits, but would open some new business opportunities and release a lone leader to become a sole proprietor without having to answer to a board. If it is a for-profit now, should it change to a nonprofit? This is a more difficult shift because people will continue to identify it as a self-serving for-profit. Can it remain a nonprofit, but shift into a social enterprise structure? Because a social enterprise prioritizes social benefits even as it operates within a sustainable business structure, such a shift should not be difficult. This would entail removing charity messaging and adding language to policy documents, including your bylaws, that emphasizes sustainable business practices that result in products for and engagement with the people your organization serves.

Take a hard look at all your branding including your logo, colors, and slogan, maybe even the name of your organization, with an eye for anything that might be misleading the people you want to attract to your organization. Do they suggest whimsy and adventure though your organization is a scholarly, academic think-tank? Are they institutional though your organization is all about radical social change? Adjustments to these brand elements, especially the name, can be quite disruptive as they signal upheaval and can cause negative results. As I mentioned earlier, a name change will sever all previous marketing and branding. It is akin to starting a new organization. So, first be absolutely certain a brand element is causing a major problem before moving forward with a facelift.

9.4.1 Dangers of Fiscal Sponsorship

Fiscal sponsorship is a false structure and deceptively easy to fall into. In the United States and some other countries, the leaders of a new organization can choose to avoid incorporating by asking an incorporated nonprofit to become their "fiscal sponsor" (sometimes called a "fiscal agent"), meaning that the established organization makes the new one part of its structure. This can look very enticing to new leaders who are already overwhelmed by all the tasks required to found an organization.

Don't be deceived! Fiscal sponsorship becomes a cozy arrangement that is difficult to escape. The most harmful problem with fiscal sponsorship is that the "mother" organization must be mentioned in all communications. Also, all checks and credit card payments that are meant for your organization must be made payable to the mother organization, not yours. This means that all of your donors, grantors, and customers will relate their experience with your programs to the fiscal sponsor. If you and your fellow leaders ever manage to break free, none of these important people will have any connection to your organization. In other words, once you break free and incorporate your organization independently, you will be starting from day number one.

The other danger is that the mother organization does all the administrative work, which allows them to take credit for sheltering your organization. They simply charge a fee such as ten percent of all income that comes in, noting your organization as beneficiary. This is fair because otherwise an established nonprofit could not justify taking on the burden of being a fiscal sponsor. Also, because of the high level of responsibility they have for your organization, you and your team will have to hand over some leadership of your organization to them.

Once you and your team have settled into this arrangement, most of you will be tempted to remain there in order to avoid the responsibility of tax returns and funder reports. I know of some nonprofits that have operated under fiscal sponsorship for more than a decade and I can easily bet they will never break free. They will also remain small. The ones I know of are either run by volunteers or have just one, underpaid staff member.

Another important danger of fiscal sponsorship is that it will limit your programs. No fiscal sponsor would take on the responsibility and administration of complex programs that aren't part of their mission. Then consider that everything that includes the name of your organization must also show the name of the fiscal sponsor in order to give full disclosure. Imagine your brochures, business cards, and website, all with two names of the organizations that run the program. We've already discussed the importance of clarity in mission and name. Fiscal sponsorship makes this impossible.

Rather than being lulled into the fiscal sponsorship trap, return to your fellow leaders and have a serious discussion about why it looked inviting. Are all of you happy with the idea of your organization staying small with very little impact—perhaps as a social club or means of networking like-minded people? Or perhaps you came together to achieve just one project. Then simply don't bother incorporating. Pass bylaws so you will have that important governance guidance, but don't feel you need to incorporate or be part of an incorporated organization. Are all of you determined to create a robust organization that makes significant long-term impact for the community you want to serve? Then realize it's time to incorporate as your own, autonomous organization. Fiscal sponsorship will only delay the inevitable and, as I described, actually undermine the launch of your organization.

The incorporation process is certainly arduous, but your pro bono attorney and accountant will be there to help, so it won't be as daunting as it may seem. I will cover how to find such pro bono helpers later in this chapter. You will need to bring them your upgraded bylaws, free of any gaps that may have caused ailments as well as some financial projections. They'll ask you lots of questions and they will have you check the drafts of forms before submitting them. As long as they have successfully assisted in the incorporation of organizations like yours, they will know the best answers to the often confusing questions posed in the forms.

My recommendation regarding fiscal sponsorship is: Don't do it! And if you've unfortunately slipped into this cozy yet dangerous situation: Get out as soon as you can.

As you embark on major structural changes keep in mind that they are the playground for rogues and factions. If your leadership team is not yet functioning well together, start with first aid and remedies to remove serious threats. Once all of you have agreed on any structural changes, you will need to capture them in your policy documents including your bylaws, your Mission/Vision/Values/Goals, and your corporate identity manual.

9.5 Policy and Procedure Upgrades

Give your policies and procedures a thorough check-through with your team. Replace brutal language with words that inspire camaraderie and empathy toward others. Remove all "lawyer speak" including all bizarre word mergers such as hereto, herewith, thereby, thereto, and so on. Nobody speaks like that, not even lawyers. Use common language. Remove all unnecessary words and redundancies. Keep your policies crisp and to their particular point.

On a similar note, don't pass any more policies than you absolutely need. When you discover a gap, rather than creating a whole new policy document, check your bylaws for an appropriate place for this addition. Bylaws are the topmost policy document on governance procedures. Any additions need to be as concise yet broad as possible. Avoid passing policies specific to unusual situations. Instead, work with your team to envision the gap that allowed your recent ailment and all other scenarios it could also allow. Your added language should block as many types of upheavals as possible. For instance, if a faction that formed through an event committee nearly tore your organization apart, don't be tempted to ban event committees. Instead, add language to your bylaws that forbids any committee from making decisions that affect the entire organization. As you add necessary language to your bylaws, also keep in mind that two-page bylaws are the ultimate goal. You may need another page or two, but don't go past four pages, to ensure that all leaders can absorb and remember their contents. Only add as many words as are absolutely necessary to state the new regulation.

Any policy documents that are separate from your bylaws may be redundant or cause confusion, so keep them to a minimum. In fact, the fewer the better. Separate policy documents that will be necessary include your Mission/Vision/Values/Goals, your annual work plan/budget, your employee manual that clarifies day-to-day operations, and your corporate identity manual, all covered in earlier chapters.

Policy documents cannot cause proper behavior. Only leaders who follow them can inspire others in your organization to do the same. So don't make the mistake of believing that once you've passed a policy the work is done. Activating policies requires a deep understanding of them and constant reinforcement for everyone who takes part in your work; from board members, to employees, to volunteers, to people who attend your events.

9.5.1 Pro Bono Attorney and CPA

You will want a trusted attorney available when needed, not only for legal advice, but to be on call in case someone tries to harm your organization. An accountant or CPA is also important for assistance creating effective management procedures.

Look for an attorney and an accountant in your community who have significant experience with organizations similar to yours—nonprofit, social enterprise, etc. Ask leaders of other organizations whether they would recommend a certain lawyer or accountant.

Once you find good ones, ask these professionals if they can donate their services. Such a professional service donation is often referred to as *pro bono*, derived from a Latin term meaning "for the public good." This will be a major donor request because these experts charge quite a bit for their services. However, most accountants and attorneys with nonprofit experience expect to serve several pro bono clients. This is a point of pride for them and something they like to report to their professional associations. But you'll still have to make a very good case as to why your organization should be one of the lucky ones they choose to serve pro bono.

9.5.2 Management Systems

Management procedures follow your chosen management system. The most common is a hierarchical system in which the executive director takes care of all other employees and directs their work. When organizations grow to more than about ten employees, they hire managers or directors per department. These managers take care of the staff members in their department and only they report to the executive director. And as I mentioned earlier, only the executive director reports to the board.

Hierarchical systems generally work well because they

ensure that everyone knows what is expected of them and who they should go to for help. This offers comfort and stability to employees. It also allows quick adjustments when opportunities or threats arise. Much like the hierarchical structure of an emergency response team, directors and managers keep their eye on the entire scene without engaging in the details and can adapt their team's tasks accordingly.

Your management system should fit the culture of your organization. For instance, collective decision making can mire some organizations into inaction. In other situations, it could enliven a small number of people with leadership skills. Such horizontal management systems where everyone has a say in every decision will always consume far more time in meetings and decision making, but if your purpose is based on this sort of interaction, you might want to consider it. Take some time to study various examples through an internet search and related books. Some variations include "flat," "network," and "matrix" management systems.

Beware of collective (or horizontal) systems if your mission is to make significant change outside of your organization. In that case, you and your team will have to act quickly and decisively, so hierarchical (or vertical) will be more appropriate. Recent adaptations of the authoritarian hierarchical model, which everyone loves to hate, have found success even in the for-profit corporate world. These new models retain the quick action of vertical management while adding various means for everyone to offer input and ideas. Such organizations operate efficiently even as they create a village atmosphere that supports and values everyone who works for them. Chances are that some of the healthy organizations you listed as examples at the start of this book follow this modern structure. Key to their success is an absence of "silos" within their operations. In other words, even with defined programs and projects that require specialists to focus on very different tasks each day, everyone working within the organization is informed about what everyone else is doing and invited to offer ideas for improvements.

Also develop your systems for inviting people outside of your organization to engage with your programs. Once they connect, capture all of their vital information in a spreadsheet or a software program made for the task and include a means of tracking their assistance on into the future. Assign someone to send out prompt thank you letters to everyone who contributes money, resources, and time. Then you will have a list of supportive people who are always at the ready to help again because you've appreciated their contributions. When you create your volunteer jobs, you can go to this list to find the people interested in that sort of work. When you organize an event, this list will be the first to receive invitations. They will also receive all of your e-newsletters and other newsworthy updates. And at the end of each year, when you send out your annual fundraising appeal, they will be the most likely to give.

Another consideration in this realm is to find a way to keep former board members and others who step down from their positions involved in your organization. Most people who step down from leadership positions do so because life throws them an unexpected curve ball. Other times, they just want a change. Don't lose these exceptional people and all that valuable experience contained in their heads. They carry the memories of your founding, of the funny experiences at your events, and even the crises you worked together to overcome. Find a means to encourage former leaders to voluntarily stay involved if they would like to. Such mechanisms can include an advisory board or a committee structure that involves former leaders.

A similar system I recommend is an exit plan for all employees who either step down or are fired. Of course if they caused immense or even illegal harm, you might not want to sit down with them. But in most cases when an employee leaves, one of the leaders needs to sit down with them before they go to find out what worked and what didn't work for them. The executive director or the leaving employee's manager is the best one to do this, though a board member could do it as well. Make sure the employee returns all materials, passwords, and other resources belonging to your organization. Then ask them about their experience as an employee. What did they love about the job? What did they hate? Ask them for any improvements they'd suggest. Someone who is leaving the organization will often feel more comfortable revealing such details than someone who is still on the job. Use this valuable information to upgrade your systems.

9.5.3 Bylaws Upgrades

Upgrades to your bylaws need to capture changes that affect the organization as a whole. If you changed the name or mission statement, these must be changed in your bylaws. Include language that sets your executive director out as equal to all board members and remove any hint of brutality.

To move away from the win or lose hostility of majority rule, consider changing to a consensus decision-making system. This does not mean that every decision will be the favorite of every leader. Consensus decision making allows every leader to engage in the discussion and results in a decision that all leaders can accept. I know from my experience working in all types and sizes of groups, that the first proposal is rarely the best. More hearts and minds are needed in order to create the most beneficial decisions, not only for the organization, but for the community it serves. Working in consensus causes the adaptation and improvement of original proposals. However, do not confuse consensus with groupthink. Respect and value all dissenting opinions, even from outsiders, and adapt your decisions to answer their concerns.

If some leaders are not comfortable with consensus alone, consider keeping consensus as the primary decision-making method and including majority voting as the means for breaking a stalemate. Even with majority voting as secondary, include clauses that require either consensus or a supermajority vote for these two actions: removal of any leader (including the executive director) and amendments to the bylaws. Then, just as with all policies, you and your team will have to actively engage these upgraded bylaws in order to bring them to life and inspire everyone involved to create the culture they describe.

Rehabilitation is not meant to be fun. The memory of the trauma is so close it haunts the entire process even as it drives it. All of you should be motivated to get through the process if only to ensure you don't ever have to face a significant ailment again.

Nutrition and exercise are a totally different story. They depend on fun. If it's not fun, it's not nutritious. Read on to learn about bringing the fun of nutrition and exercise into your organization and everything you and your team do together.

Chapter 10
Nutrition and Exercise

Now that you and your team have pulled your organization through the tough work of diagnosing and treating your ailments, it's time to develop and adhere to healthy habits so you won't have to go through such an ordeal again. Nutrition and exercise for your organization may sound boring, but the fact is that if they are indeed boring, they are not nutritious and do not count as exercise. This is one difference between healthy habits for people and those for organizations. People will actually benefit from choking down bland food as long as it is loaded with nutrients. We will also benefit from planting ourselves on a treadmill for ninety boring minutes. Not so for organizations, where boredom is the death blow.

Everything you do from here on should be fun, even your board meetings. Bring cookies. Meet in a park. Invite family members and even pets to join all of you for a picnic after the meeting. If you're a bicycle organization, go for a bike ride after the work is finished. Make playful activities an expected part of your leadership gatherings.

As every leader comes to expect fun, injecting fun into the programs, products, and services you offer to your members, clients, and customers will also be expected. If it's not fun, find something to add. Can you add a riddle to your e-newsletter? What if you expanded it to a mystery series that revealed a different clue each month and rewarded those who guessed correctly at your annual fundraising event?

Even your campaigns can be fun. One of my favorite examples of a fun campaign was led in 2010 by a small group of young people in a rundown suburb of Dallas, Texas called Oak Cliff. Their vision of their neighborhood was quite different from the grey empty buildings lining the high-speed streets where the sidewalks had been cut back to tightropes. After looking into why their neighborhood was so ugly, they discovered pages and pages of cryptic city ordinances abolishing every imaginable element of a friendly street including fruit stands, flower boxes, and even window awnings. The only hint of explanation for these arcane laws was an overzealous effort many years before to stop people from loitering. But beautiful streets invite loitering and that's exactly what these young folks wanted their streets to do. They gathered a bunch of their friends, passed the hat to raise several hundred dollars, and over a few months gave two blocks in their neighborhood major, though temporary, makeovers.

For the first project, one of their city council members had implied it was okay so they obtained a permit to close part of the street. That was all the approval they needed. For both projects they painted bike lanes and crosswalks, lined the streets with potted plants and trees lent to them by local businesses, blocked the middle of one street with more potted plants, opened temporary businesses in the vacant shops, and set out borrowed furniture as cafe seating in the newly expanded sidewalk area. They even made copies of the ordinances they were breaking and attached them to the pertinent street elements.

Hundreds of people showed up to each of the weekend events to stroll along the beautified streets where cars now had to crawl along at a snail's pace. Several city officials joined in the fun and were shocked to see their ordinances attached to such lovely street improvements. These awestruck residents, officials, and visitors sipped beverages at the pop-up cafes and bought art made by local artists in hastily assembled galleries.

Less than four years later, these streets in Oak Cliff are

known as the bicycle streets of that area and real cafes and art galleries have moved into the vacant storefronts. The potted plants have been replaced with planted trees and all the residents in the area are proud of their revitalized neighborhood. Also, as you can guess, all of those ridiculous city ordinances have been repealed. Another significant result of these wildly fun weekend initiatives is that the original group of young people went on to create a full-blown, healthy international organization that is now helping communities all over the world take charge of their neighborhoods. Check them out for lots of inspiration at BetterBlock.org.

10.1 Attractiveness

Better Block is an excellent example of a healthy organization. The reason I know this is that people flock to it—not just in Oak Cliff, but from cities and towns around the world. The leaders' schedules are booked with speaking engagements and there's a waiting list for their consulting services. Better Block is a very attractive organization.

Attractiveness is certainly a goal of any nutrition and exercise regimen, but for organizations it should be primary. Unless people flock to your organization you will be susceptible to ailments. New energy, new ideas, ways to help; people bring the nutrients necessary for health. During your diagnosis and treatment efforts, you will have discovered reasons why people have not been attracted to your organization. Now it's time to make it attractive. Injecting fun is a major part of this. But also look at other ways people perceive your organization. Make adjustments that present it as professional and up to the task of achieving your mission. Look at your website, the exterior of your office, the interior where all of you work. Are these attractive and inviting to the people you want to take part in your organization?

All of you as leaders will also be on display. Show your constituents that you are having fun even as you tackle tough initiatives. Build your team spirit and pride in your organization and put them on display. The Better Block leaders took on an immense campaign, one that would be too daunting for most people. Can you imagine demanding that your city allow such audacious changes to a street in your neighborhood? And yet they succeeded, not by attending endless meetings or complaining to officials. Instead they chose a fun way to demonstrate how ugly and dangerous their streets had become. People will always be more attracted to fun methods than to mundane demands void of vision.

Some people will not be attracted to your organization, especially when you work toward significant social change. Anyone who is benefiting from the status quo will oppose your work. Opposition is actually a compliment. It means that what you are doing is meaningful. Focus instead on making your organization attractive to people who should support it. By doing a perfectly fabulous job you will even win over some of those opponents.

As you make these attractive adjustments, keep an eye out for that all-important balance between the energy your organization is consuming and the beneficial energy it gives out. You'll need to raise enough funds to pay for your initiatives, but don't obsess over money. Consider whether partnering for the items you need will have a better impact than simply paying for them. Better Block raised only several hundred dollars for their initiative. All the plants and beverages came from local businesses they partnered with. All the furniture, lights, art, and other decorations came from individuals who wanted to help. Each of these items came with a person. Those people continue to help the organization. They are also the ones who established the permanent trees and fixtures and opened the new businesses along the streets. If the Better Block leaders had spent all their time raising money to buy all those items, they would have missed the opportunity to engage all of these important people.

10.2 Breathing: Getting the Word Out and Receiving Feedback
Proper breathing is critical to any exercise regimen. Too

fast and heavy and you'll pass out. Too little and you'll run out of steam. This goes for organizations as well, where communication is how they breathe. Pace your communication so people won't get sick of hearing from you but will also not forget about you. Make your communications so dazzling they grab your audiences and don't let go until the entire message is delivered. Everything you send out has to stand out amidst a constant barrage of advertising that competes for attention. Look for messages from other organizations, even ads and commercials that capture your attention. Tap their methods and avoid those that bore you or cause you to turn your attention elsewhere.

I was delighted by a recent e-marketing campaign sent out by an organization I used to work for. Splore is a nonprofit in Utah that takes people on outdoor adventures who might not otherwise have such an opportunity. Their clients include people with physical and mental disabilities as well as people who are in difficult situations that prevent them from taking part in activities like river rafting, rock climbing, and cross-country skiing. I was one of their river guides throughout the 1980s and could tell endless stories about the triumphs and achievements of the people we brought along on those wilderness river adventures. As far as I knew, back in those days all of our energy was focused on producing exceptional outdoor experiences for the people we worked with. It wasn't until recently that I started noticing their bulletins and e-newsletters. Some made me giggle, others sparked my interest so I'd open them to read about their latest outdoor pursuits.

Then I began receiving a battery of Splore emails just days apart. The first one had a subject line of "Rock climbing is bad for kids." After opening it I read, "Said no one. Ever."

"Kids Should Stay inside."

Said no one. Ever.

Below that I found links to photos of kids rock climbing and a nice description of what they were calling their Fall FUNd Drive to raise money for particular equipment upgrades along with a clear list of the needed items. The next had a subject line of "Kids should stay inside." Then came one with "Get high with Splore." That one opened to a photo of people rock climbing and this quote from one of their clients from their veteran's program: "I got to the top of the climb and I cried. I'm 75 years old and I didn't know I could still do that." Yeah, by then I was crying, too; and looking forward to the next. It arrived with "Volunteering sucks" and a return to "Said no one ever" inside along with a photo of happy people frolicking on a river raft and an overview of Splore's volunteer program. The last one was "For a good time call..." and inside a photo of guides and clients acting silly at one of our hilarious polyester parties on a river trip and a confirmation that Splore is indeed all about good times.

There were five in all and as they progressed, they counted down to the end with an increase in urgency to give. Each included a huge, convenient DONATE button. A few weeks after it was over I received one more email from them with a subject "You made our day" with a similar theme inside and a shower of appreciation for everyone who helped make the fundraising campaign a success.

Make your breathing exercises constant and delightful with an eye for spontaneity and fun such as Splore used in their e-marketing campaign. Your messages should carry the face as well as the heart of your organization as they capture the hearts of current and new helpers alike. Celebrate your accomplishments without overstating them.

Even as you create delightful external messages also look at the channels you are using to deliver them. Add as many channels as you possibly can. If you're only using Facebook, you're missing an enormous number of people who are either not signed up or are tired of using it. Don't forget the people who have no access to computers. Low-income people generally rely more on paper flyers, door hangers, and word of mouth. Connect with neighborhood leaders so they can spread the word for you. Many older people prefer to receive paper copies in the mail. These can also be useful handouts along with your usual brochure at any event. Hold your own events that welcome everyone. Find regular excuses to send press releases to all the media in your area. Keep your website updated with your latest happenings. Create as many communication channels as you possibly can and keep them flowing.

Include in all of your external communications a means for people to communicate back to your organization. In fact, think of them as two-way breathing, out and in. Show appreciation for any feedback so your reputation as an open, inviting place will spread. Ask people in your community what they think of your organization, even if they haven't yet engaged with it. Listen for the level of effectiveness your programs are reaching and whether there is room for improvement. Especially listen for any harm you might be causing and make corrections immediately. By opening the channels of communication you will not only find a means to deliver your messages, you will also encourage your constituents to communicate how they feel about your work. This information is vital nutrition for the health of your organization.

10.3 Nutrition through Fundraising

Funding alone is like refined flour compared to the whole grain nutrition of living, breathing donors who bring their talents and experience. People build and become the muscles of the organization. If you sit in your office all alone typing up grant proposals and shoving them out a narrow mail slot, you will never tap the full nutritional value that fundraising offers through connection with your donors.

Before you begin any fundraising effort, make sure your long-term plans and your annual work plan/budget are ready for show time. These documents will contain the answers to common questions funders might ask and will give you what you'll need to complete comprehensive funding proposals. Seek out as many diverse sources of funding as possible. This will prevent funding emergencies caused by the loss of any particular funding.

All fundraising is people giving to people. Whether you are asking your aunt for a donation or writing a ten-page grant proposal, the most important element of any funding request is your personal connection to the people who will decide whether or not to give. So, for all your grant proposals, all your sponsorship requests, and all your government contract applications, do your best to first connect with the decision makers. This personal connection will set your proposal out from the others they receive and it will give it a better chance of success.

Set up several methods for donors to give to ensure you've included their preferred method of donating. The longer it takes for a donor to figure out how to give to your organization, the more likely they are to change their mind. The three most common donation methods are online by credit card, mail-in form for check (post this online for them to print and use it as a handout), and hand delivery. Include a form with each that captures the donor's full name, their mailing address, email address, donation amount, and the date they donated. A phone number is also a good idea in case there's a problem with their donation. Then enter all of this information into your donor and helper tracking system and follow it up with a letter of appreciation that specifies the amount they gave and notes your organization's tax-deductible status for their records.

10.3.1 The Direct Ask

The direct ask is the simplest type of fundraising. You find people who are passionate about your organization's work and simply ask them for a significant donation. However, while it is simplest logistically, it can actually be the most difficult. Few leaders jump for joy when given the opportunity to make a direct ask of a potential donor.

By asking potential donors for a donation, you are offering them an opportunity to contribute significantly to their community.

Most people have every second of their lives scheduled. Your suggestion to give is their opportunity to make a real impact by supporting the work of your organization. They make the donation to enable you and your team to help people and their community— work they simply could not do themselves.

So first, change your mindset from asking for help to offering donors an opportunity to help their community. They can't say "yes" unless you ask. And if they feel appreciated, they are likely to give a donation year after year, as long as your system reminds you to ask them again. One of the top reasons donors stop giving is because no one asked them to give again.

Before reaching out to a potential major donor, check that they are likely to be interested in your organization's work. Have they supported similar programs in the past? Perhaps they volunteer at a like-minded partner organization. Do a bit of research to find out what level of contribution they have given in the past.

Once you have done your research on your potential donor, it's time to prepare for the initial call. Have all your planning documents in front of you to answer any questions they might have. Practice describing why you contribute your time and money to your organization so you can demonstrate your own commitment. This initial call is not the time for the funding request. The only request you will make here is for them to meet with you to discuss their financial support of your organization.

At the meeting, ask questions so you can learn this person's hopes and dreams and how they would like to invest their money in the community. Briefly interject details about your organization and align these details with this donor's needs, but let them do most of the talking so you can learn their desires.

Make your request just before the meeting is over, connecting it with their desires, but be clear that the money will be used for your organization's current, planned needs. (Remember: never "chase the money," that is, go after inappropriate funding that would throw your organization off track.) Include a specific amount, taking into account the research you did on their previous contributions and financial ability. Also take note that you could be meeting with a property owner, a business owner, an expert, or someone who could donate needed supplies. Your request could be for services, supplies, or a property donation, so don't get stuck on monetary donations. Consider any "in-kind" donations that would fit your work plan for that year.

Send a handwritten thank you note by the next day no matter what their answer was, simply thanking them for the meeting. Even if they did not choose to donate this time, they might change their mind in the future. This note is separate from any additional written details they may have requested. After you receive their donation, immediately send a professional thank you letter, which they can use for their records.

Show appreciation for their donation where appropriate. These general accolades and communications such as print and email newsletters, advocacy alerts, event notices, and such, add to the substance of your relationship with this donor. But these gestures do not replace your direct, personal connections with them. Always make room in your schedule for direct contact with your major donors, even if it's just a personalized update on their favorite programs. Such updates show them you value them as a partner without asking them too often for a donation. One request per year of each major donor is plenty.

Also, look for special ways to involve donors. This could include asking for their advice or personally inviting them to an event or ribbon cutting that includes their interest. Once you get the knack for the direct ask, you'll find that you enjoy connecting with these folks because they share your passion and appreciate your showing them how their contribution is helping your organization's work. And remember: Ask them again next year! If you don't, they'll be disappointed, maybe even insulted. Donors want to give. Give them that opportunity by asking.

10.3.2 Fundraising Events

Fundraising events require a tremendous amount of time and resources, so don't take one on unless you and your team are sure of success. They do bring one important benefit that none of the other fundraising methods have—gathering important people together to help your organization. Great events can solidify donors' commitments to help your organization. Your donors have fun, they learn more about your organization, they meet all the leaders, and they see their colleagues and friends also offering their support. This can be very powerful for long-term relationship building. But every event also comes with a serious risk: if it flops, the potential donors who do attend will leave with a bad impression of your organization and, as I mentioned earlier, they are even more likely to spread a bad report to their friends and colleagues. Take this risk seriously and before moving forward be sure you and your team can pull off your event.

Successful fundraising events always have talented people at their helm. Be sure that someone on your team possesses the unique quality necessary to host an enchanting event. Don't move ahead until you've received such a commitment, especially from someone who has led fundraising events in the past. Besides the event coordinator, you will need a team of helpers tasked with various specialties depending on the type of event you are planning.

As you and your team discuss your event plans, differentiate between social events and fundraising events. This is a fundraising event, not just a social event. Each of you should understand this distinction and ensure that all of your promotional messages clearly state it. For instance, if you want to hold a bike ride to raise funds, call it a fundraising ride, not just a fun ride or social ride. The same applies for a dinner. You need the people who attend to expect to donate. If your ride or dinner is filled with people who just want to have fun, the event will cost your organization money rather than raising funds. Social events are certainly something to consider adding to your plans, but don't expect them to generate funding.

No matter what sort of event you organize, charge a ticket price well over the amount needed to cover all costs, assuming you sell your minimum (you'll need to do a detailed event budget to know this amount). This will ensure that your ticket sales cover your event costs and that the rest of your fundraising tools during the event actually bring in money. Describe your current programs to show what donations will go toward. If your event includes an auction, realize that typically only ten percent of attendees will bid, so you will need several more ways for attendees to donate. Perhaps add a raffle and games they pay to play. Lay a donation envelope on each plate so quiet attendees will have a comfortable means of donating. Offer as many ways to contribute as you can.

Any fundraising event requires a minimum of six months to plan and prepare; one full year is better. Gathering your helpers, securing the event location, promoting the event to people who can afford to donate, and organizing the supplies, speakers, and food take an enormous amount of time. Just as with your other planning procedures, take the time to list all the necessary people, supplies, and steps you'll need to succeed. Then carefully place these in a conservative timeline that allows for setbacks. You'll see that six months will be pushing it.

Before starting your effort, do thorough research into the type of event you would like to organize. Seek out event planners in your community who can offer ideas. And don't forget to track down that all-important, energetic event coordinator well in advance.

10.3.3 Sponsorships

Sponsorship is just a fancy form of advertising for companies. As advertising has become a constant blur in all of our lives, companies have learned that their advertising money is better spent associating their brand with nonprofits and social enterprises. They expect to pay, usually from their advertising budget, so charge an appropriate amount.

Research sponsorship levels of other nonprofits in your community and either round down or up depending on how your organization compares to theirs. Potential sponsors need to know exactly where their logo will be seen and by whom. They only care that their particular potential customers see their logo and learn about their company's support of your organization. For instance, if your organization protects marine animals, a cruise ship company might like to see their logo on a banner on your boat and at your events where many people interested in the ocean will see it. But they'd likely have little interest in their logo hanging above the pool for sea lion recovery where only staff and active volunteers will see it.

Always give sponsorships a time limit. If you're requesting sponsorships for an event, perhaps your fundraising event, let them know that the promotions with their company name and logo will only show through the event's conclusion. For general sponsorships, limit the display of their company name and logo to a year because you want to ask them again each year.

Place their logo in appropriate places that do not overshadow your organization's branding. For instance, if you want to display them on your website's home page keep sponsor logos small, below yours and to a minimum. Banners, T-shirts, printed materials, and inclusion in a press release and newsletter article are all appropriate for sponsor mentions and logos.

Requesting sponsorships is just like the direct ask, except this is a business deal. Do the research, then request the meeting. You will be asking for a portion of their advertising or marketing budget. A potential sponsor will need to know specifics about your organization and the audience that will see their logo. Before arranging the meeting, honestly assess the value of sponsoring your organization. How many people recognize your organization and know what it does? Is your organization's reputation truly good in the eyes of this sponsor's target customer base? Do you have multiple channels for displaying their name and logo? If you and your team can confidently answer these questions in the positive, sponsorships are likely a good addition to your fundraising portfolio.

When you meet with a potential sponsor, in addition to all your planning materials, bring along details such as:

- Where their logo will be displayed and for how long,
- The demographics of the people who will see their logo and why they are likely to buy their products,
- Details about the work of your organization and how their sponsorship will help.

The best book I have found on the topic of sponsorships for nonprofits is *Made Possible By: Succeeding with Sponsorship* by Patricia Martin. She covers everything nonprofits must do to compete for sponsorships including nonprofits with multi-million dollar budgets. Even though much of the book will not apply to smaller nonprofits, understanding the expectations of sponsors will help any leader make appropriate sponsorship requests.

10.3.4 Grants

Foundation and government grants are the most compelling way to raise funds because they seem to be less time consuming than other methods and can end in the receipt of a big check. Unfortunately, there's a lot more to it.

Grant writing is not much different from the direct ask because you must do that early research to understand the foundation's needs, how much they typically give, and their preferred way to receive a request. But grants lack the most important part of the direct ask—direct connection between you and the funder. In fact, over the years most foundations have erected massive barriers between themselves and grant seekers. I suppose this is simple survival. With about 1.5 million nonprofits registered in just the United States alone and only 120,000 foundations in the country to absorb their requests, the odds are stacked against every proposal. This ratio is similar around the world as the number of nonprofits grows, so all foundations are barraged with funding proposals. On top of this, grant-writing consultants spent the last decade telling rooms full of nonprofit leaders that the best way to get their proposal funded was to personally speak with someone at the foundation. To protect themselves from the onslaught of phone calls and requests for meetings, foundations have shut off all contact with grant seekers. Many no longer accept proposals unless they have personally requested, or "solicited" one.

This extreme competition coupled with the lack of personal contact makes grant writing a long shot. You can only hope for ten percent of the proposals you write to be funded, and this assumes that each of these absolutely perfect proposals went to likely funders.

On the lucky chance that you personally know a decision maker at a foundation or government agency, approach them by following the direct-ask concepts I described earlier in this chapter. With this personal connection, such a grant proposal becomes that ideal person-to-person connection. However, once this person gives you the thumbs up to submit a proposal, you will still need to follow the foundation's proposal guidelines exactly because your buddy is likely not the only person to review it.

Government grants and contracts might also be worth considering, especially if your organization plans to take on a significant local project. Note that government contracts are different from government grants as they align more with a business agreement than simple provision of funds. Both arrangements still benefit from a personal connection, then require an immense amount of paperwork before they are approved.

While I caution against high expectations for grants, I still recommend including grant writing in your fundraising activities. First learn the common procedures of grant writing from books and local workshops. Talk with grant-writing experts in your community to get a full picture of this process. Then do all the preliminary work necessary to ensure you find the grantors who are most likely to fund your organization.

Creating a grant-writing system will save you valuable time. The first piece of the system should be a grant template that includes essential information about your organization that you will want to use in all proposals. Next make a spreadsheet of the funders you plan to approach. As you proceed with your applications, add to the spreadsheet your results from each one. This system will help you avoid reapplying to unlikely funders and keep track of any deadlines the grant-makers may require of you.

10.3.5 Crowd Fundraising

Crowd fundraising combines the ease of online giving with the comprehensive project presentation of grant writing. As I write, Kickstarter.com is by far the most popular site and the one I would recommend for a very defined project. IndeGoGo.com is another, but does not have the visitor traffic of Kickstarter. I recommend studying the latest reviews of crowd-funding sites before choosing one. Be sure to compare the numbers of successful projects and amounts raised.

Success for any crowd fundraising campaign starts by ensuring that your project fits your chosen site's guidelines, then preparing your video and page material well in advance so it will stand out. You'll also need to clean up your outreach lists before you launch your campaign so you can send your pleas for donations within a tight timeframe that conveys a sense of urgency. Thirty days should be plenty. In order to succeed in thirty days, you will need all of your promotion tools sharpened and ready as soon as your campaign goes live. Study similar successful campaigns and use them as a model.

10.3.6 Indirect Asks

There are many methods of asking for donations indirectly—mass mailings, emails, press releases, website appeals, online fundraising challenges through other sites, Facebook, and other social media. None of these will bring in significant funding, but don't skip them. Make them a backdrop of your fundraising that promotes your organization's need. Not only will they bring in small donations, they can also reach your potential major donors, sponsors, and grantors before you approach them, familiarizing them with your accomplishments and adding to their confidence to give.

To increase your chances of success with mailings and email appeals, spend quality time building and updating the list of people who will receive them.

10.4 Exercises for Health Gains

Every healthy organization follows regular exercise routines that channel energy into effective activities and bring in nutrients. I've covered many of these already, including effective management, productive meetings, and assessment of achievements.

Sometimes necessary exercises can seem daunting. Seeking out criticism is one example. In order to fully connect with the community you expect to serve, you need to exert some energy connecting with people who have contrary views. Though their views may anger you personally or even be delivered disrespectfully, hold back your emotion and listen respectfully. By listening to them you will learn invaluable details about how people outside your comfortable circle feel about your organization. These people may have significant influence over your potential helpers and donors. They are the colleagues, classmates, neighbors, hairdressers, mechanics, and business owners who your supporters chat with every day. They may not step up to help, but a passing word of approval can go a long way. Their perception will be clear and honest, not draped with the enthusiasm of support. Open as many channels as you can to invite and welcome people to offer concerns and ideas for improvement.

Of course, inviting criticism can also bring unhelpful nastiness, so set in place strong rules of conduct for your feedback systems. If you use an online public forum, install a CAPTCHA form that blocks spammers from abusing it. Assign an administrator from your organization to screen all posts so blatant malice and offensive language will not be posted. Require online posters to include their full name and contact info along with an email confirmation method that holds their message until they have responded from that address. These steps should block malicious messages while allowing constructive, nutritious criticism.

Set in place similar rules for in-person feedback so that you will shield your staff and volunteers from attack. Train your team to help people deliver more useful criticism with a goal of helping. In case you add public forum events to your palette of feedback routines, start each forum off by creating meeting rules with attendees.

Combine this outreach for feedback with your internal discussions. Give everyone on your team many channels through which to offer feedback, ideas, and complaints, even anonymously if needed. The people on your team are the ones who go to bed at night thinking about the organization. These active minds are the most likely places for the best ideas to grow.

As you seek nutrients from many points of view you will find value even in bad behavior. Take the time to examine what motivated someone to lash out or act inappropriately. Some of my favorite examples of this are graffiti arts programs that invite outlaw graffiti artists to create public art. These innovative programs do not dismiss these young people as lawbreaking gangsters. Instead they recognize them as packed with energy, creativity, and talent. By setting clear rules in place first, these programs are able to guide budding artists through the creation of murals and other projects that beautify rather than harm their communities. Along the way the programs also teach community stewardship as well as business development to inspire young artists to create their own, sustainable art projects. Programs like this are taking place in Dallas, Texas; Philadelphia, Pennsylvania; and Oakland, California.

Closer to my home there's been a recent spree of illegal trail building by mountain bikers in Sedona, Arizona. They caused significant damage to vegetation and archeological sites. Forest Service officials fined all the offenders, banned them from the forest, and are threatening to throw some in jail. I can't help thinking about all that eager energy to build trails and improve mountain biking in that area. They certainly need to be punished and held accountable for their crimes, but can't this be done in a more productive way? The Forest Service could have harnessed the riders' enthusiasm to build better trails designed for the environment that also fill an obvious need. These mountain bikers know exactly what their community wants to see for their sport.

Before lashing out at or dismissing bad behaviors, look deeper to discover why the offenders spent their energy as they did. You might just find a way to shift their energy into something positive. By doing so, you will cause two positive outcomes: helping someone move out of bad habits and the creation of something that benefits your community.

Capture all of these various ideas into a useful form that can be referenced during your board meetings and annual planning. Keep your project-management and planning routines intact, including following your agreed-upon work plan/budget for that year, but create the space needed to develop new ideas and projects that can be launched in the future. Controlling all this new input also requires you to stay on top of your overall management and bookkeeping routines so that new ideas won't derail your current efforts. This will protect your current projects and programs as you bring in the nutrients necessary to keep them healthy and growing effectively.

Involve your entire leadership team in all of your fundraising and outreach efforts. Some might enjoy the backstage work like compiling lists of people or researching grants. Others might be more social and enjoy event planning. Just be sure that every one of your fellow leaders takes on an important role in your fundraising and outreach. Not only are the core leaders of any organization the best at inspiring others to connect, donors will recognize and appreciate this commitment from the leaders.

Don't forget to have fun. Connecting with people and raising funds for important programs should be an industrious and enjoyable venture. This enthusiasm will spread and build momentum as more and more people want to take part in your success.

Now let's look at some of the equipment that can inspire such effectiveness.

Chapter 11
Equipment for Effectiveness

You and your team will gather all sorts of great equipment to assist your exercise efforts. Your Mission/Vision/Values/Goals document as well as your annual work plan/budget will help you keep an eye out for useful devices. These can include actual equipment like tools, computers, and software as well as training mechanisms and curricula that will guide members of your team.

An organization called KaBOOM! offers a great example of successful use of equipment to accomplish their goals. They are a national nonprofit in the United States that helps struggling neighborhoods build playgrounds. While I love their emphasis on playground equipment, it is not the equipment that most impresses me about their work. It's their systematic planning approach for each neighborhood they work with. This approach is so effective that after several months of following their comprehensive step-by-step online planning process, a local group builds their own playground in just one day.

Other sorts of healthy exercise equipment can include materials for planning and training, toys in the office that remind workers to have fun, team T-shirts for volunteers to instill a sense of pride in the projects they work on, and devices like blind folds and wheelchairs for employees to learn what it's like to be disabled. Choose equipment that will accelerate your work and inspire your team to effectively strive toward your mission.

Next I'll offer some of my favorite tools for effectiveness to give you an idea of the many sorts of effective equipment you and your team can tap.

11.1 Priority Matrix

The Priority Matrix on the next page is a useful tool for distinguishing between critical work that the organization relies on and urgent tasks that require immediate attention. Critical work is always best done well before it becomes urgent. And urgent work that is critical must be kept to a minimum to keep stress levels low and prevent programs from being compromised. The matrix shows how to avoid spending all your time in critical/urgent mode by keeping your staff and fellow leaders working ahead of deadline and not scrambling after tasks that should have been done yesterday. Make panic a rarity.

I especially like its emphasis that 100% of volunteer work must be in the not-critical category because non-leader volunteers should never be placed in a position where the organization's success depends on them. They are still placed in the urgent section because volunteers are fabulous for helping make current projects even better.

Use this matrix during planning meetings or to show others where time is likely being wasted. For instance, if someone is defending work that is not contributing to your current programs, show them the matrix and ask them where their work fits. Chances are they will see that they have been wasting time on busy work.

Find a printable version of the Priority Matrix on the One Street website at OneStreet.org under Management in the left menu.

One Street's
Priority Matrix

Critical

Critical, Urgent

~ 15% of staff time

- Responding to unexpected crises
- Filling in for staff pulled away by emergencies or suffering burnout
- Dropping everything else to meet last-minute deadlines
- Explaining to donors, partners, members and clients why responsibilities weren't met
- Cutting back planned expenses to make up for missed income

Critical, Not Urgent

~ 85% of staff time
(also board time, but only at the governance level, not daily duties)

- Developing and following a clear work plan and budget for each year
- Ensuring all clients are served well and more feel comfortable coming to the organization
- Preparing important activities well in advance
- Submitting reports, payments, proposals & other important paperwork well before deadline
- Communications with members, clients, supporters, staff, and volunteers to ensure all are updated on news and activities.
- Seeking out and meeting with new partners and funders
- Developing potential new opportunities.

Urgent

Not Urgent

Not Critical, Urgent

~ 100% of volunteers' time
~ Any staff time saved by avoiding crises

- Member/client inspiration & gathering ideas
- Mailing tasks
- Event decorations and other creative activities
- Data input
- Promotions distribution
- Grant and funder research
- Surveys
- Spreading the word about the organization & inspiring others to get involved

Not Critical, Not Urgent

~ 0% of anyone's time

- Distractions that have nothing to do with accomplishing the organization's mission
- Personal activities that should wait for personal time
- Random web browsing
- Busy work

Not Critical

11.2 Business Plan

A business plan is not necessary for most nonprofits, though it is a necessary guide for all for-profits as well as nonprofit social enterprises. If you are leading a nonprofit that has no product sales, your Mission/Vision/Values/Goals document will suffice for long-term planning. However, any entrepreneurial effort you undertake will benefit from the addition of a business plan. Simply creating a business plan will force all of you to think in a sustainable mindset and the plan itself will become a fundraising tool for the creation of products and services you anticipate selling.

This plan will detail the demographics of your community, show income potential, and reveal expected costs for encouraging people to buy your products and services. I use the word expected because no business plan can replace the careful oversight needed from your team once your program is launched. A business plan will need an update every few years, especially in the beginning, to compare your projections with actual accomplishments. From these comparisons, you will see where more energy and resources are needed and you'll find those surprising elements that succeed far beyond expectations.

While your business plan will serve as an important internal planning tool, think of it mainly as a marketing tool. It can be a leave-behind for meetings with potential partners and funders. For instance, imagine approaching an owner of a property that would be perfect for your community center. Following the direct ask steps, you want to ask this owner if he or she would consider either donating their property for a tax write-off or leasing it to your organization at a very low rate. This is a big request! Bringing along a professionally prepared business plan that outlines how your program will succeed can mean the difference between a breakthrough and a disappointment.

There are many resources on the internet and at your library that will show you how to create a strong business plan. I've seen single-page business plans and ones that would break a sturdy table. Err on the shorter end of this spectrum. Just as with your bylaws and all your other planning documents, make your business plan concise and easily understood. Even so, take note of these sections that are commonly expected in every business plan:

- Executive summary
- Business description (include mission, vision, values, and goals in narrative)
- Business location with pertinent details
- Market definition including competition
- Products, inventory sources, and services
- Organization and management including pertinent bios of leaders
- Marketing and sales strategy
- Financial management (include your first year's budget and planning)

One of the easiest tools I've found for roughing out a business plan is the Build Your Business Plan template on the U.S. Small Business Administration's website. Once you have filled in each section, you and your team can refine your plan and take it to a professional printer for final design and printing. Spend the extra money to make it look professional. You won't have to print very many, so it won't pinch your budget too much.

11.3 Effective Campaign Planning

An effective campaign planning process streamlines social-change efforts. Campaigns are different from programs because they are meant to strike at a problem, make the needed change, and end in triumph. Perhaps it's a new law or the abolishment of an unjust law. It can also mean the approval of a new project such as a dog park or street redesign that invites novice bicyclists. Programs, on the other hand, are meant to continue and even grow as long as they are beneficial.

No campaign plan can get past step one without a comprehensive understanding of the problem the campaign is meant to solve. In the case of the dog park project, the problem might be that many families have no place to take their dogs for leash-free romping. This alone would likely not persuade city officials to bother with the project, so the problem would have to include concerns pertinent to those particular officials, perhaps a stagnant real estate market that does not attract families because there is no place for their dogs to play.

In every campaign planning workshop I have led over the years, defining the problem takes an extraordinary amount of time. People don't like to be negative. My workshop attendees always want to jump to solutions without dwelling on problems. But you cannot develop a solution without fully understanding the problem it is meant to solve. The dog park problem could note decreasing real estate prices and the solution could include real estate sales figures from other cities before and after investing in dog parks.

There's a brief overview of an effective campaign planning process posted on the One Street website; look in the left menu, under Campaign Planning. Effective campaign planning includes choosing a winner, budgeting, and managing the campaign. Assume that your campaign planning will take longer than expected. You should not publicly launch a campaign until the planning is complete. Pull your fellow leaders together along with anyone you believe can help with that particular campaign, and focus everyone on defining the problem from the perspective of those with the power to make the change. Don't let them jump to solutions or tactics until the problem definition work is done. Write out concise descriptions of the problem, solution, tactics, and management steps. Give each of your fellow leaders a copy so you will all have the same expectations as the campaign unfolds. Your campaign plan will be an internal document, but it will offer many of the sound bites and talking points you can use in your campaign materials and media releases. Set a reasonable timeframe, with an expected victory party date. Keep to the schedule and do everything you can to make it happen.

Assuming you win the change, leverage your victory party with a press release, perhaps even a press conference alongside any supportive officials, and seek out interviews through TV, radio, print, and online. Work it! Campaign victories are hard to beat for creating a buzz. Even if you lose, you can still leverage the result by showing how much more work your organization must do to make this change. With a touch of drama and intrigue, even a loss can attract lots of media attention and thus more helpers. Then adapt your original campaign plan for your phase-two attempt and go at it again.

11.4 Innovation Diffusion Game

Innovation diffusion explains how a new idea, product, or activity spreads (or doesn't spread) throughout a population. At the start, only the innovators participate. Then the early adapters try it out and finally the mainstreamers jump in and the new thing becomes ordinary. Causing innovation diffusion, on the other hand, is a much more complex process that very few people understand and many would pay dearly to master. Imagine if every new product became an expected item to buy. We'd all be out of money and buried in junk. So in a way it's a good thing that innovation diffusion retains a bit of mystery.

This is a major concern for organizations working for social change. Any change or product you and your team bring forth needs to reach full diffusion throughout your target community in order to succeed. You can read many books and websites about innovation diffusion, but you will never find a better tool for understanding how it works than this unpolished, little-known game called the Innovation Diffusion Game. Find the instructions here: www.context.org/iclib/ic28/atkisson or simply search "Innovation Diffusion Game." All you need is one person to prepare the game, a large yet quiet room, and about 20 willing participants, each of whom will play an important role. Some will be mainstreamers, others reactionaries and laggards. The innovator will have to rely on change agents in order to reach the mainstream people. There'll be a curmudgeon and a spiritual recluse who will actively block the innovation. I've organized this game in countless settings over the years and it never fails to impress. You'll find instructions for preparation on that web page as well as the role descriptions.

The game only takes one hour including the debriefing session, but will change the perspectives of participants on what it takes to create social change. You and your team will gain terminology to remind each other to ignore curmudgeons and focus instead on finding your change agents within your community. Most importantly, you will replace anger with empathy for behaviors you previously thought bizarre. We all play different roles depending on the innovations we encounter. Ever since I first played this game, I have watched myself step into every role outlined in the game. I've been a curmudgeon and reactionary against bicycle helmet-law proposals. I've been a laggard when presented with new technologies yet been an innovator of new products, programs, and perspectives. I've enjoyed being a mainstreamer as I came late to new initiatives underway in Prescott, most recently an effort by a local tennis association to rebuild our public courts.

Find the game, play it with your team, and I promise it will open a whole new realm of perspectives. If you are the organizer, it will take about one hour to set it up including finding the right room, printing and cutting out the roles that people will pick randomly, and inviting everyone to show up at your chosen time. The game will be finished within one hour. You'll be amazed at the ratio of effort to inspiration.

11.5 Concentric Circles

I often use concentric circles to show leaders what might be hindering their efforts, especially when their best supporters are vanishing. This doesn't mean best *monetary* supporters because most organization leaders understand these folks need special care. The people I'm talking about are more easily forgotten: your founders, the people who first stepped up to help even when your logo looked like a road-killed aardvark, your former leaders, the networkers who tell everyone how great your organization is, and anyone who would drop whatever they were doing if you asked them to help. I call these folks the core of the organization.

For some reason, leaders of rapidly growing organizations tend to forget their core. They connect with a major funder or launch a campaign with a huge partner and turn all their focus into that narrow channel, discarding activities that kept their core people involved.

Other times I've found fragmented planning efforts such as burdensome strategic planning or strengths/weaknesses/ opportunities/threats (SWOT) assessments as the cause of such abandonment. An isolated planning process or SWOT assessment can easily point to specific concerns out of context; for instance, that the organization must persuade people outside their normal demographic to become members. With such an ultimatum in place, staff could turn all membership development and communication toward these unlikely people and forget to keep current members actively involved. One of the best signs of health for organizations is when they have managed to persuade unlikely people to support their work, but this is *always* accompanied by unceasing and lavish attention given to core supporters.

During such discussions with leaders, rather than trying to describe this core and outer reaches with words, I grab a blank piece of paper and pencil and draw concentric circles. I point to the center as the place where their core people reside. This certainly includes themselves and their fellow leaders, but also all those great folks who would jump to help without having to be convinced the organization is worthy. The core also includes your most committed customers and clients.

Then I explain that inside the second ring is where most

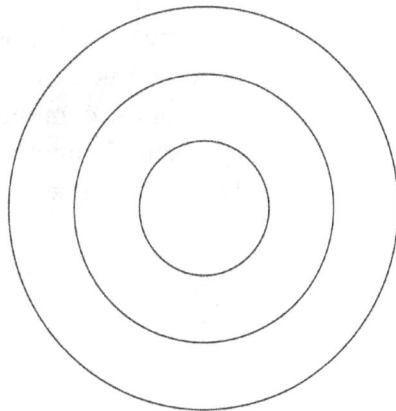

supporters and potential supporters reside. These are folks who might give a bit of money each year or show up for an event as long as absolutely nothing else is going on. They like the organization and totally support its work, but do not prioritize assisting it. I think I'm in the second ring for our local tennis association.

The third ring out and farther is where the rest of the population resides. They are folks who couldn't care less about your organization. They may even be active opponents.

You always want your outer rings to move toward your core and perhaps even join it. Building your core is critical. But the farther you reach away from your core, the more energy it will take to persuade even one person to make the move. Meanwhile, at the center, your core people are buzzing, ready to help. Say the word and they will be there. The amount of energy it takes to engage your core is tiny compared to the energy needed to draw an outer-ring person to even attend an event. Yet so many leaders take their core supporters for granted, ignore them, and finally wonder why they no longer show up to help. Core supporters vanish just like anyone who feels abandoned. And once they are gone, they will join the outer ring people and will be just as difficult to persuade to help, if not more so. Once dissed (short for disrespected), no one wants to repeat the experience.

Never diss your core. They will disappear and leave your concentric circles hollow like a donut. Donut organizations are very unhealthy because the only people engaged in their work are people who don't much care about the organization. Avoid the donut by keeping the communication channels open to your core supporters, personally inviting them to gatherings and events, and ensuring they can easily engage in all the activities that interest them.

Concentric circles are a handy way to understand people problems so you can keep your core people happy and ready to help.

Now that we've looked at all these nutritious and healthy habits, it's time to move on to our final chapter: Preventing Ailments. Preventive measures are a much better way to spend your energy than having to respond to ailments.

Chapter 12
Preventing Ailments

There's an old saying that prevention is the best medicine, but you cannot prevent something you do not understand. That's why this chapter is last. Anyone who used this book to diagnose and treat an organization ailment will now be an expert on their particular ailment. Even if you read it without facing trouble, you will have a well-rounded idea of the causes of these problems. This newfound expertise will give you the confidence to quickly reverse even the slightest deviation. You can now hold your mission statement up as an all-encompassing diagnostic tool to discover ailments. Whenever you and your team cannot focus all your energy on accomplishing your mission, you will know without a doubt that your organization is ailing. This shows you why your mission statement needs to be short and perfectly concise—not only to guide everything you do, but to alert all of you when something is wrong.

People will always be your greatest assets even as people are the most common causes of organization ailments. Leadership requires a complex understanding of these dynamics. You can now make intricate distinctions between behaviors that previously might have appeared identical. Someone with an opposing viewpoint is different from someone actively trying to do your organization harm. You can now welcome and value contrary ideas as you find ways to improve your programs so they appeal to a variety of people. From another perspective, you should now feel uncomfortable whenever group discussions are short and do not question a proposed decision. Until you and your fellow leaders examine all angles of a major decision, including alternatives, you will not know whether it is the best possible way forward.

By now you should clearly see the danger of groupthink— that affliction when group members do not think critically, but simply go along with the group in order to avoid being ostracized. Prompt contrary viewpoints, integrate input from outsiders, and empathize with your opponents during your leadership discussions. You may return to the original proposal or improve on it. Either way, your commitment to full analysis of every major decision, including alternative courses of action, will prevent groupthink disasters.

The benefits of proper planning as well as communicating intentions both internally and externally should now be clear. Opposition is expected when you propose a major social change, but not from the people who should back it. You can now distinguish your opponents from your supporters and even your mild supporters from your all-important core. When opponents articulate their concerns, you can find value in them. But when factions threaten to tear your team apart, you can confidently respond to stop that bad behavior.

You should now recognize the value of contrary viewpoints, whether they come from outsiders or even from your own gut when you sense your activities are no longer reaching the level of significance intended by your team. KaBOOM! offers another good example here because they are no longer satisfied with just building playgrounds. Darell Hammond, founder and CEO of KaBOOM! wrote with dismay in the Fall 2013 edition of the *Stanford Social Innovation Review* that their activities were missing the point. Building a playground in a day was so impressive, that was the only message that was being spread through the media. In fact, KaBOOM! had been founded to bring the importance of play back into the lives of children in the United States. According to the article, titled "When Good Is Not Good

Enough," their playground program had captured lots of attention that resulted in 2012 being their best financial year, but even so the leadership team knew something was wrong. As Mr. Hammond put it, "We couldn't continue to ignore that many playgrounds are empty most of the time, active play is disappearing in America, kids are spending more than eight hours a day in front of a screen, and that almost half of all kids living in poverty attend schools that don't offer recess."

Their decision to shift direction was not easy because it meant venturing away from a sure winner, that focus on building playgrounds that guaranteed a flow of income and endless positive media attention. Yet they knew this work was not serving their mission with the needed impact. They set to work to refine their public image and put in place a clear goal that would shift expectations away from impressive playground construction to high-impact advocacy for play. Their website still offers their renowned system to sign up for a playground, thus retaining the goodwill and inspiration from their earlier work. At the same time, according to the article, they have set a new goal in place: "*All* children, particularly the 16 million children living in poverty in the United States, get the play they need to become successful and healthy adults." That goal is not dependent on playgrounds. Instead, it has sent their team into advocacy discussions with lawmakers and school administrators, the decision makers who have the power to reshape whole communities into places where all kids can play whether there's a playground or not. Now that's what I call a self-aware and healthy leadership team, one that is willing to shift away from guaranteed funding and accolades into new territory to ensure they reach their mission most effectively.

While you and your team might not need to make such a difficult shift, you can now use your mission statement to start the diagnosis of any ailment. You can also expect your leadership team to work together toward that mission, welcoming and incorporating contrary views, but never fracturing to work against each other. With this team spirit and expectation to achieve significant change, you can even empathize with those who behave badly. This is not easy, especially after struggling through a crisis caused by someone who tried to harm your organization. After considering the many ways good people are drawn into horrible acts, you should have gained the insight to understand their digression and not hate them for what they did.

Do not confuse empathy with the swift action needed to remove someone from a role that allows them to inflict harm on your organization. People placed into improper roles that do not match their talents, skills, and passion are likely to do very bad things whether intentional or not. Now you can remove them immediately—with confidence, empathy, and even respect—as you inform them that it's time to leave. Of course now you will have policies in place that will help prevent mismatched placements and, when one occurs anyway, those policies will back up your decision and show the offenders why their removal was necessary.

The culture and principles of your organization should shine through all of your policies as you and your fellow leaders bring them to life. Fun can now permeate everything you do. Fun keeps your best leaders happily at the helm. Fun keeps your core supporters coming back to help. And fun bursts through your public image to make your organization attractive to even the most unlikely supporters. Healthy organizations are attractive. They exude a come-hither attitude that makes people smile and stop what they're doing to find out more. Their name, colors, slogan, website, and all of their external communications beckon anyone and everyone to take a look. Everything they say and do is wildly interesting yet totally honest and not overblown. Everything they say they did, they actually did. And they know how to flaunt it.

Even as you develop your new, attractive strategies the process should make you smile. Unless you and your fellow leaders are giggling, the ideas are not fun enough. Keep working at that fun until your organization is so attractive it makes all of you blush. Leading an extraordinary organization is supposed to be fun and it should make all of you very happy. Happiness is the ultimate state of good health and because organizations are people, an organization can achieve health only when its people are happy.

Fun and happiness shield against ailments much as our immune system does. An opponent could feel quite justified in setting out to harm an organization that spends its days at infighting, but attempting to disrupt an organization where people enjoy their work would just be weird. The same goes for someone placed into an improper role. They may be miserable and frustrated, but with everyone around them having fun, sabotaging the organization would likely not occur to them. They would more likely choose to voice their frustration, which could lead to a productive discussion and finding a better role for them. They might also choose to leave, which could be the best choice for everyone.

Even an authoritarian, charismatic leader will be repelled from a healthy, happy organization. Such leaders are catalysts for brutality and groupthink atrocities. They need to rule over meek subjects who lack confidence and vision. A team that is working effectively and laughing together will be a barrier to someone expecting to use the organization for their own agenda, so they will look elsewhere.

As you laugh and play together, celebrating significant accomplishments toward your refined mission statement, keep this comforting thought in mind—that ailments and diseases that regularly plague organizations are bouncing right off your protective shield of fun and happiness.

Leadership is a delicate responsibility. We all cringe at the atrocities caused by authoritarian dictators all over the world. It's easy to write off these dictators as lunatics, but just as I have stressed empathy for anyone behaving badly, a closer look will give us a disturbing shot of reality. Every leader, every one of us, is susceptible to becoming a dictator and causing enormous harm. As you buttress your organization with fun and happiness to keep out such dictators, also look at yourself and the rest of your team. When an organization finds its groove and can approach officials with significant proposals that are ultimately approved, there is a danger of its leaders becoming intoxicated with their newfound power.

Power easily poisons humans and thus the organizations they lead. Everything becomes effortless. All you have to do is demand something and your wish is granted. How many fairy tales have been written around this theme? A genie's lantern, a magic wand, a flittering fairy, a snap of your fingers and you get exactly what you want. Humans are terribly lazy so we lust after this very thing even though most of those fairy tales warned us of the danger of this tendency. The best leaders remember they are human and that they are just as susceptible to becoming a destructive tyrant as anyone else. They also know that the people they are leading must take an active role in bringing about the changes they propose, that dictatorship does not pass as true leadership. One of my favorite quotes in this regard comes from Lao Tzu, who lived in the 6th century BCE:

> "The wicked leader is despised by his people. The good leader is loved by his people. The great leader causes his people to say, 'We did it ourselves.'"

We have to work at not being wicked. Then it takes even more work to set aside our ego to give everyone involved the credit they deserve.

Honestly assess the progress toward your mission. Remember the star analogy and how easy it is to slip into red giant behavior. Just as an individual leader can morph into a tyrant, a healthy organization can turn into a red giant. With all the busy work and false accolades popping around a red giant, its distracted leaders simply miss the fact that nothing is being done toward their mission. Their fiction mesmerizes them as they grab at funding and steal credit for work they did not do just to feed their ravenous organization.

Make impact analysis part of your ongoing procedures to

ensure you are not patting each other on the back for contrived accomplishments. If your mission is to plant and care for street trees, count how many you planted each year and how many you fed, watered, and pruned. This may seem obvious, but I'm afraid too many organizations don't bother. It's much easier to *claim* accomplishments than actually analyze them. I also discover many organizations that repeat reports of accomplishments they completed years ago void of new data. Analyze your current accomplishments and, if they are not significant, your organization is ailing and you need to return to the diagnosis and remedy steps in this book. Only measurable change toward the mission justifies the energy consumed by an organization.

Constantly monitor the health of your organization, not only the impact of your work, but the way your team is communicating. Communication in an organization is parallel to the ABCs of medical first aid: airway, breathing, circulation. When communication stops—either within your team or to your community—something is terribly wrong. Respond immediately.

As you look for danger signs you will also discover tangible products for your communications. Just because you have become a sensitive and watchful guardian of your organization doesn't mean you can't have fun with it. Not only will you come up with exact numbers to quantify your accomplishments, for instance the number of street trees you planted, you will also catch delightful details you most likely would have missed otherwise. Capture the jokes and pranks, the zany ideas and outlandish proposals that result from welcoming everyone to contribute. Bring your communications to life with these stories of working and laughing together.

These are the stories of your journey together through the raging seas of controversy and battle, the struggle to pull your organization out of danger, and the triumph of achieving your goals as a team. Each of you is living this drama because you are a team. You are privileged to have this opportunity. Most of your supporters will never have the chance or even desire to step into the tumultuous leadership role. Share your stories with them so they can taste your triumph and offer to help even in a small way. Through their contribution they will know the triumph is theirs.

We've come to the end of our journey together examining common organization ailments and their treatments. Now you and your team can take it farther. With good health, that balance of energy inward and outward, that tantalizing attractiveness, any organization can shift ugliness to beauty, oppression to dignity. Preposterous dreams can become expected missions. Now it's time to unshackle your dreams and see where they lead.

Let's build this vigilance for all organizations working to help our world. We can no longer accept the ailments that have engulfed so many. Health is now a choice. I have offered you remedies that I have enjoyed over many years of challenging these ailments. I know they work, yet so few people even know there are remedies much less hold an expectation to save a struggling organization. My hope is that as readers of this book use these remedies to save worthy organizations, other remedies will be developed and along the way that coveted expectation for beneficial organizations to thrive will finally become the new norm.

I'd very much like to hear how you used this book to help your organization or expanded on the ideas I presented here. You can reach me directly at: +1-928-541-9841, sue@onestreet.org or Skype: sueknaup

For more information about One Street or to purchase more copies please visit: www.onestreet.org.

Recommended Resources and References

ORGANIZATIONS and WEBSITES:

- Better Block:
  www.betterblock.org
  - o consulting for street improvements

- Friends of the River:
  www.friendsoftheriver.org
  - o river protection in California and beyond

- GuideStar:
  www.guidestar.org
  - o list of nonprofits in the United States

- Idealist:
  www.idealist.org
  - o global network and resources for nonprofit organizations

- Innovation Diffusion Game:
  www.context.org/iclib/ic28/atkisson
  - o interactive game that demonstrates social change

- KaBOOM!:
  www.kaboom.org
    - advocating active play in the United States

- Marin Humane Society:
  www.marinhumanesociety.org
    - Animal sanctuary and adoptions in Marin County, California

- Milgram obedience experiments:
  www.en.wikipedia.org/wiki/Milgram_experiment
    - overview of Milgram's disturbing experiments and their results

- One Street:
  www.onestreet.org
    - global support, resources, and services for bicycle organizations

- Splore:
  www.splore.org
    - outdoor adventures for people with disabilities or disadvantages in Utah

- Stanford Social Innovation Review:
  www.ssireview.org
    - social innovation resources

- Tech Soup:
  www.techsoup.org
    - software discounts for nonprofits in the United States

- Wildcare:
www.wildcarebayarea.org
    - o   Wildlife rehabilitation and public education in the Bay Area, California

BOOKS and MOVIES:

- *12 Angry Men* (movies 1957 and 1997)

- *The Crisis Caravan: What's Wrong with Humanitarian Aid?*, Linda Polman, Picador, 2010

- *Dead Aid: Why Aid Is Not Working and How There Is a Better Way for Africa;* Dambisa Moyo; Farrar, Strauss and Giroux; 2009

- *The Effective Executive in Action*, Peter F. Drucker and Joseph A Maciariello, Collins, 2006

- *The Ethical Executive: Becoming Aware of the Root Causes of Unethical Behavior,* Robert Hoyk and Paul Hersey, Stanford University Press, 2008

- *Inventing the Nonprofit Sector: and Other Essays on Philanthropy, Voluntarism, and Nonprofit Organizations*, Peter Dobkin Hall, Johns Hopkins University Press, 1992

- *Invisible Man*, Ralph Ellison, Random House, 1952

- *Lord of the Flies*, William Golding, Faber and Faber, 1954 (also movie 1963)

- *The Lucifer Effect: Understanding How Good People Turn Evil*, Philip Zimbardo, Random House, 2007

- *Made Possible By: Succeeding with Sponsorship, a Guide for Nonprofits*, Patricia Martin, Jossey-Bass, 2004

- *Mistakes Were Made (But Not by Me): Why We Justify Foolish Beliefs, Bad Decisions, and Hurtful Acts*, Carol Tavris and Elliot Aronson, Harcourt, 2007

- *Obedience to Authority: An Experimental View*, Stanley Milgram, Travistock Publications, 1974

- *The Ox-Bow Incident*, Walter van Tilburg Clark, Random House, 1940 (also movie 1943)

Acknowledgements

This book would have suffered a sad end many years ago had it not been for a valiant group of writers who waded through my early misfires. In late 2009 and well into 2010, this writers' critique group was my first sounding board as I struggled to find a shape for the book. Joe DiBuduo, Nancy Owen Nelson, Irene Blinston, and Karen Despain delivered their solemn assessments with kindness and hope, showing me the rare bits that would inspire organization leaders. I can't thank you guys enough for your long-suffering patience. Alas, the vast majority of rubbish I dragged you through has fallen to the delete key, but you will certainly recognize the gems you picked out. Thanks to you, they have blossomed into this final result.

Once the book took on a somewhat readable appearance, I knew it still had a long way to go. Marianne Vaiana was the first full-length reader. I still wonder how you kept your cool all the way through our hours-long lunch meeting as you calmly repeated the cuts and rearrangements needed to guide a struggling leader through its content. Thank you for standing your ground even as I pleaded for release from such a painful reworking. You saw its needed shape as I was stuck in the details.

The next readers also deserve medals of valor as the scars still showed from the major surgery after Marianne's recommendations. I'd pieced it back together, but needed new eyes to determine whether it was finally whole and flowing well. Kaethi Diethelm (who carried it along on a bicycle touring vacation!), Steven Ayres, Johanna Hawley, Paul Simpson, and Karen Nozik gave it their expert assessment and all returned with serious concerns. Each of you showed me where it dragged or jumped ahead and then forced the reader to flip back for needed information. Because of your effort, I spent weeks rethreading and in the end had cut fifty pages of unnecessary babble. You guys found the gaps and snags that led to a far more enjoyable read. Thank you.

The last two readers, Barbara Jacobsen and Jerry Hiniker, gave me the long-awaited thumbs up. You have no idea what a relief it was to receive your praise and accolades. You two were my green light that set me on the hunt for our wonderful editor.

When John Hopkins answered my call for an editor I was a bit stunned as I'd worked with him for many years when he was leading the Green Mobility Network in Miami. I'd forgotten he had also been the editor of one of Miami's top newspapers. I couldn't have imagined a better fit for the job. John took great care as he moved word-by-word through the book even as he offered suggestions from the perspective of an organization leader.

In August 2014, 47 generous people backed our Kickstarter campaign to fund the publication costs. Robert Milligan had once again made an excellent video telling the story for the campaign. Your contributions carried the book past its final hurdle and into publication.

Thanks to each and every one of you for seeing and believing in the value of this book.

I also must thank the stars of this book—all the leaders of organizations I have met and worked with since I was a youngster. There is no way I can list all of you here. I only hope you see your contributions in these pages and know the pride of protecting your organization to continue its important work. Without you this book would have no content. Thanks also to the readers who will use its contents to save great organizations. Without you this book would have no purpose.

Index

www.ingramcontent.com/pod-product-compliance
Lightning Source LLC
Chambersburg PA
CBHW070542200326
41519CB00013B/3097